WITHDRAWN

D1547889

MILTON & WORDSWORTH

By the Same Author

THE BACKGROUND OF ENGLISH LITERATURE

CROSS CURRENTS IN ENGLISH LITERATURE OF
THE SEVENTEENTH CENTURY

ESSAYS AND ADDRESSES

CRITICISM AND CREATION

✻

In collaboration with J. C. Smith

A CRITICAL HISTORY OF ENGLISH POETRY

✻

In collaboration with Sandys Wason

THE PERSONAL NOTE

✻

Chatto & Windus

MILTON & WORDSWORTH

Poets and Prophets

A STUDY OF THEIR REACTIONS
TO POLITICAL EVENTS

BY

SIR HERBERT J. C. GRIERSON
LL.D., LITT.D., F.B.A.

*Emeritus Professor of Rhetoric and English Literature
in the University of Edinburgh*

1950
CHATTO & WINDUS
LONDON

PUBLISHED BY
Chatto & Windus
LONDON

❃

Clarke, Irwin & Co.
TORONTO

First published in 1937
Second impression 1950

CONTENTS

Preface   vii

CHAPTERS

I. Prophetic poetry; the Hebrew Pro-
phets   1–25

II. John Milton and the Renaissance
theory of poetry; a poem "doctrinal
to a nation"; the awakening; the
"reform of reformation"   26–47

III. The first shock; marriage and divorce; a pause in pamphleteering and
return to poetry; the first decisive
step; regicide   48–64

IV. The dismissal of Parliament; Milton
and Cromwell.   65–82

V. The final return to poetry; Milton's
early poems; *Paradise Lost*; its doctrine and its temper; the prophetic
and the poetic in the poem; Milton's
diction and verse   83–131

VI. *Paradise Regained*; Milton's Christ;
Samson Agonistes; Milton's final vindication of himself and those he followed
in the great deeds of the Rebellion   132–146

VII. Wordsworth and the French Revolu-
tion; a contrast with Milton   147–182

References to Quotations   183–185

PREFACE

THE lectures here printed were given as the North-cliffe Lectures in Literature at University College, London, in the early spring of last year; and, with some modifications and additions now embodied, as the Turn-bull Lectures at Johns Hopkins University, Baltimore. I wish to thank both these institutions for the opportunity afforded me. My desire was, starting from my own conception of what prophetic poetry is, and illustrating that from the greatest of all prophetic poets, to trace the developement of Milton's thought and feeling from the time that, moved by the events of the years following his return from Italy, and rapt in a vision of a regenerate England, he definitely conceived of himself as one on whom also a burden was laid, and looked forward, as his share in the sacred task, to the composition of a great poem that should be "doctrinal to a nation". Was that design fulfilled in *Paradise Lost*? Or was that poem, with the two which followed, the statement of the conclusions to which he had been driven by a gradual disappointment of his hopes and a loss of faith in the human will? Is *Paradise Lost*, in part or whole, a prophetic, intuitional, poem in the sense I have tried to illustrate from other prophetic, intuitional, poets? It was with a view to emphasise this last question that, after beginning with the Hebrew prophets I have ended with Wordsworth. He too began with a vision of "human nature born again", and he too was disillusioned. But whereas Milton's final pronouncement seems to me to be the expression of a conclusion reached by a conscious deduction from his experiences (not excluding the effects of certain prejudices which had their source in the cast of his mind and the character of his education), Wordsworth's deepest convictions, whatever their content and worth, were reached intuitionally, prophetically. They, or their expression, were later modified occasionally by a super-induced orthodoxy, but with this I am not here concerned.

In tracing the development of Milton's mind I have wished to understand him. This can only be done by trying to sympathise with what was best in his impelling motives; and I may have given the impression of being more in accord with him than I am. I have in an elsewhere published volume played the part of *advocatus diaboli*. But, I confess, it offends me to hear Milton, or for that matter Luther or Calvin, dismissed confidently as "a bad man". The final Judge of Men, if a more searching, will be also a juster judge than his little self-constituted vicegerents on earth.[1] To me there is both

---

[1]   "But Gertrude, lily, and Luther, are two of a town,
          Christ's lily, and beast of the waste wood."
                                        Gerard Manley Hopkins.

"Don't like what you say of Milton, I think he was a very bad man: those who, contrary to our Lord's command, both break themselves and, as St Paul says, consent to those who break themselves the sacred bond of marriage, like Luther and Milton, fall with open eyes into the terrible judgement of God." Hopkins to Robert Bridges.

Milton, as a matter of fact, did not break the bond of marriage, though his wife endeavoured to do so by deserting him. But Hopkins did not share his admirers' and disciples' contempt for Milton as a poet: "The choruses of *Samson Agonistes* are still more remarkable: I think I have mastered them and may some day write on the subject.... His achieve-

greatness and nobility in the disinterested passion and unwavering consistency with which Milton followed the spirit whithersoever it led him in the pursuit of a pure religion and a well-ordered state. The impression he left on those who knew him is well expressed by Heimbach in 1667: "Certainly I, who admired in you less individual virtues than the wedding of differing virtues, not only revere in you many other things but also that you have achieved a blending, rare and beyond the desert of this age, of gravity (which your countenance, right worthy of a hero, displays) with the most unruffled courtesy, of charity with sound judgement, of piety with statesmanship, of statesmanship with vast learning, and, I add, of a highminded and by no means timid spirit (even where younger men have faltered) with a solicitous love of peace." I am too old also to have sympathy with a criticism of Milton's poetry which might be applicable to Young's *Night Thoughts*. To censure Milton's style because later poets affected it for purposes quite other than his, used it as a stilt to elevate their lesser stature, seems to me not unlike censuring a cathedral because it does not afford a good model for the building of flats and bungalows. We have passed, indeed are still passing, through a period in which it is hard to judge a poem like *Paradise Lost* aright. When we have escaped from the wish either to defend or criticise his cosmology and history and theology we shall see it as a great utterance of a great soul in a great but troubled age.

ments are quite beyond any other English poet's, perhaps any modern poet's."

I should like in closing to thank Dr J. C. Smith, C.B.E., for the care with which he has read my proofs and made suggestions for improvement that went much beyond correction of occasional errors of the press. My debt to him on this account is but a small part of what I owe him, during an acquaintance now of many years, for conversations on many and various topics from which I at any rate have derived both information and fresh insight.

H. J. C. GRIERSON

January, 1937

NOTE

IN writing the following chapters for delivery as lectures I had not troubled to note minutely the sources of my quotations and I have in printing supplied these somewhat loosely. I thought it well, therefore, for the help of any critic or student wishing to verify, to give a list of my quotations from Milton, the Bible, and a few other works. The extracts from Wordsworth will be readily traced

CHAPTER I

Prophetic Poetry—The Hebrew Prophets

THE revival of interest of late years in the poetry of
the so-called "metaphysicals" of the seventeenth
century has led to much critical discussion of the connection between the content and the form in poetry, or,
more strictly, between the intellectual element of statement and reasoning in the content and the sensuous and
imaginative pleasure which we derive from the diction,
imagery, and rhythms of poetry. The favourite phrase
is "unified sensibility". We are told, a little pontifically, that this unified sensibility was disturbed by the
great influence of Milton, so that the natural medium
for the expression of our thought has become exclusively
prose, while poetry, I suppose it is contended, became
the expression of feeling, of thought only in so far as this
had become crystallised as the representative of some
mood of feeling. Ratiocination, argument, was in romantic and Victorian poetry deemed out of place as
proper only to didactic verse, and that, after the experience
of the eighteenth century, stood condemned. I am
stating the contention as I understand it, not ratifying
it. It is not of course the first time that there has been a
protest against poetry which seemed devoid of thought,
of content. This was, I think, the objection of Johnson
and Goldsmith to the poetry of the school of Gray and
other writers of Odes and Elegies:

The truth is I take up books to be told something new; but
here as it is now managed the reader is told nothing. He opens

the book and finds very good words truly, much exactness of
rhyme, but no information. A parcel of gaudy images pass on
before his imagination like the figures in a dream; but curiosity,
induction, reason, and the whole train of affections are fast
asleep. The *jucunda et idonea vitae*—those sallies which mend the
heart while they amuse the fancy—are quite forgotten; so that
the reader who would take up some modern applauded per-
formances of this kind must, in order to be pleased, first leave his
good sense behind him, take for his recompense and guide bloated
and compound epithet, and dwell on paintings, just indeed because
laboured with minute exactness.

"What oft was thought but ne'er so well expressed"
had become "What ne'er was thought but yet is well
expressed". Whether Goldsmith's objection to the
poetry of his own day is the same as Mr T. S. Eliot's to
the poetry of Milton and the next two centuries is
doubtful, if I am aware of exactly what they mean by
this "unified sensibility" and its pervasive presence
in the poetry of the metaphysicals and absence in all later
poetry.

For any discussion we must start from some common
basis, and that is the fact that poetry is an art whose aim
is to give us pleasure by the manner in which a thing is
said, i.e. it may be in despite of the disagreeable character of what is said in satiric and realistic poetry; or in
disregard of the trifling, commonplace character of what
is said, "What oft was thought etc."; or again it may be
in addition to the interest and moving power of what is
said, so that the beauty of the expression affects us like
that beauty of the body which, Aristotle tells us, is the
flower of health and strength, the pleasure which
"perfects the activity".

Now to take "What oft was thought etc.", there is a mass of poetry in which the common sentiments of humanity, or of some division of humanity, or some epoch in the history of human civilisation, finds in the words of the poet expression in a way that delights readers. Such poetry abounds, representing various levels of culture and experience, from simple ballads and songs to the odes of Horace. Gray's *Elegy in a Country Churchyard* is a shining instance in our own literature: "The Churchyard abounds with images which find a mirror in every mind, and with sentiments to which every bosom returns an echo." It is superior to a ballad, according to the same critic, because it appeals alike to the vulgar and the learned. "*Chevy Chase* pleased the vulgar but did not satisfy the learned; it did not fill a mind capable of thinking strongly. The mind of Shakespeare was such as the ignorant could take in and the learned add nothing to." These dicta of Dr Johnson show that the poetry which gives us "What oft was thought etc." is not necessarily devoid of thought. It will awaken trains of thought in the reader varying in depth and range according to his own mind and experience, but such poetry will not invite its reader to follow a subtle train of reasoning, of ratiocination. It deals in accepted conclusions, the echo to which in one mind and another may be the same in essence but vary enormously in range and reverberation:

> Aequa tellus
> Pauperi recluditur
> Regumque pueris, nec satelles Orci
> Callidum Promethea

Revexit auro captus.   Hic superbum
Tantalum atque Tantali
    Genus coercet, hic levare functum
Pauperem laboribus
    Vocatus atque non vocatus audit.

To-morrow and to-morrow and to-morrow
Creeps in this petty pace from day to day,
To the last syllable of recorded time,
And all our yesterdays have lighted fools
The way to dusty death etc.

Like such poetry on the great inescapable experience of death, love poetry is apt to move round through a limited range of thought, voluptuous, tender, passionate, melancholy.

But there is poetry in which the poet thinks, reasons, argues, and this ratiocination is an integral factor, as well as the form, i.e. diction, imagery, verse, in the total effect. But here again there is a difference between certain varieties of poetry into which ratiocination enters that deserves consideration, for I am not sure that it is clearly envisaged by all those who at the present time are talking of "unified sensibility". Take what we call "didactic poetry", poetry which elaborates an argument, a disquisition, which might be developed in prose, the *De Natura* of Lucretius, *The Pleasures of Imagination*, *The Art of Preserving Health*; or take a more oratorically developed thesis, Dryden's *Religio Laici* or (here mingled with some narrative) *The Hind and the Panther*. What is common to these is that it is the argument, the intellectual thesis, which comes first. It is his interest in *this* which has induced the poet to attempt the making more clear, at least more attractive, his exposition of it by giving to it poetical decoration and metre. He may feel that this is a difficult undertaking. Even Dr Johnson found it difficult to conceive of good poetry in Dyer's *Fleece*: "How can a man write poetically of serges and druggets?" "The woolcomber and the poet appear to me such discordant natures that an attempt to bring them together is to couple the serpent with the fowl." But this is a criticism of the subject, not of the argumentative evolution. Dryden, who is probably the greatest master of argument in verse, yet feels that the strictly argumentative parts must not be too poetical:

> Yet this unpolished rugged verse I chose,
> As fittest for discourse and nearest prose.

It is in the digressions, the flights of feeling and imagination, that Lucretius or Dryden is most poetical. But there is another way in which ratiocination, argumentative developement, may come into poetry, which is illustrated by the so-called "metaphysical poetry" of the seventeenth century, and by other poems also, notably some of Browning's lyrics, as *The Last Ride Together*, that strange poem *Too Late*, and many others. In such poems it is the feeling which comes first. It is in seeking to give expression to an intense and possibly complex mood of feeling that the poet developes a subtle, argumentative strain of thought, using it may be this or that philosophy which is current at the time, scholastic with Donne, or psychological to-day. As I have said elsewhere:

The thought in the poetry is not the primary concern but the feeling. No scheme of thought, no interpretation of life becomes for Donne a complete and illuminating experience. The central theme of his poetry is ever his own intense personal moods.... His philosophy cannot unify these experiences. It represents the reaction of his restless and acute mind on the intense experience of the moment, a reading of it in the light now of one, now of another philosophical or theological dogma or thesis...developed with audacious paradox, or with more serious intention, as an expression, an illumination of that mood to himself and to his reader.

Dante and Donne have in a special manner achieved this kind of effect. They brought into poetry, Dante quite seriously, Donne sceptically, the subtle, syllogistic argumentation characteristic of the scholastic philosophy. This is the idea really conveyed by the term "metaphysical", which might just as well be "scholastic"; poetry not only full of *concetti metafisici ed ideali* but subtly ratiocinative in its evolution. This is the poetry which Mr Eliot and his school have in view when they speak of "unified sensibility", thought that feels and feeling that compels to think. It is this interaction of thought and feeling, expressed in a language "such as men do use", which they accuse Milton of having disintegrated. But of that I will speak again when I come to deal with Milton's diction and verse.

In the meantime I want to emphasise the fact that there is yet another way in which thought may enter into poetry than by either the subtle ratiocination of the "metaphysical" or the common "topics" of the poet who wishes to win immediate effect. There is poetry in which the thought is neither a process of ratiocination nor yet the echo of the thought and feeling of the society in which the poets live, the civilisation which has shaped their minds and hearts. What poets of this kind have to say comes from the depths of their own thinking and feeling, and it may profoundly shock and startle the people to whom it is addressed. But the poets who thus speak advance no arguments, communicate nothing of "the discourse of reason" by which they have reached their conclusions. They simply announce them as truths of which they have no doubt, but which it is laid on them to proclaim from the housetops, to cry aloud in accents of warning or denunciation. The thought which comes from within comes with such force, such unpremeditated compelling power, that it seems to them to come objectively from without, at times in voices and visions, as when Isaiah saw God sitting amid the Seraphim or Joan of Arc saw Catherine and Michael on her right hand. And the voice must be obeyed:

O Lord, thou hast enticed me and I was enticed; thou art stronger than I and hast prevailed; I am become a laughing stock all the day.... If I say I will not make mention of him, nor speak any more in his name, then there is in mine heart a burning fire shut up in my bones, and I am weary with forbearing and I cannot contain.

It is thus, I understand from recent writers, that revelation is understood by many theologians to-day.[1] The mind of man cannot discover God, but God reveals himself to the prophet in suprarational convictions, from which he may then reason and reach not infrequently wrong conclusions though from true and thus revealed premisses. I have no intention of disputing this doctrine.

[1] Ernest Scott, *The Idea of Revelation in the New Testament*, 1936.

I believe that all great ethical and spiritual truths come from God and that by way of great individuals.

"The conversation", Eckermann tells us, "then turned upon the *Antigone* of Sophocles, and the high moral tone prevailing in it: and lastly upon the question—how the moral element came into the world." "Through God himself," returned Goethe, "like every thing else. It is not a product of human reflection, but a beautiful nature inherent and inborn. It is more or less inherent in mankind generally, but to a high degree in a few eminently gifted minds. These have by great deeds or doctrines manifested their divine nature; which then by the beauty of its appearance won the love of men, and powerfully attracted them to reverence."

There is, Goethe goes on to point out, a secondary morality:

A consciousness of the worth of the morally beautiful and good could be attained by experience and wisdom, inasmuch as the bad showed itself in its consequences as a destroyer of happiness both in individuals and the whole body, while the noble and right seemed to produce the happiness of one and all. Thus the morally beautiful could become a doctrine and diffuse itself over whole nations as something plainly expressed.

Such gifted and noble spirits were the great Hebrew prophets, and so they were able to proclaim new and startling spiritual truths:

I hate, I despise your feasts, and I will take no delight in your solemn assemblies. Yea, though ye offer me your burnt offerings and meal offerings, I will not accept them: neither will I regard the peace offerings of your fat beasts. Take thou away from me the noise of thy songs; for I will not hear the melody of thy viols. But let judgement roll down as waters, and righteousness as a mighty stream.[1]

[1] Amos v. 21–4. Revised Version, and so in all the quotations.

And it is from such a depth of unreasoning conviction that there wells up a cry like Wordsworth's:

> The soul that rises with us, our life's star,
>   Hath had elsewhere its setting and cometh from afar etc.

But a poet who writes in this manner is clearly not one who is content to give fresh and beautiful expression to the thought and feeling of the society in which he lives; nor yet does he, like Lucretius or Dante, seek to give poetic expression to a body of articulated doctrine which has gained his allegiance. The prophetic poet starts from no articulated scheme of philosophy, no stereo-typed theology. The great Hebrew prophets deal in no proofs of the existence of God. "As Jehovah lives" (i.e. as certainly as that is a fact) "that is the one and only article of the old religion of the people of Israel." So Duhm in *Die Theologie der Propheten*. From that they start. Their message is not that God exists, for no one disputes that, but that he is a God of righteousness and mercy who hates the cruelty and the licence of magical nature cults.

> Wherewith shall I come before the Lord, and bow myself before the high God? shall I come before him with burnt offerings, with calves of a year old? Will the Lord be pleased with thousands of rams, or with ten thousands of rivers of oil? shall I give my firstborn for my transgression, the fruit of my body for the sin of my soul? He hath shewed thee, O man, what is good; and what doth the Lord require of thee, but to do justly, and to love mercy, and to walk humbly with thy God?[1]

Justice; Mercy; and Resignation to the Will of God. That was the vital message of the prophets, not the

[1] Micah vi. 6–8.

predictions which they drew as inferences from their first principles and from the facts of history unfolding themselves before them—drew sometimes rightly, sometimes wrongly.[1] When Bishop Burnet converted Lord Rochester he laid great stress on the

prophecies in the Scripture where things were punctually predicted some years before their completion, not in dark and doubtful words uttered like the oracles which might bend to any event, but in plain terms, as the foretelling by name that Cyrus should send the Jews back from the captivity.

We do not think now that Isaiah in the eighth century foretold by name the doings of Cyrus in the sixth. Few things did more harm at the Reformation than the interest taken in the predictive, apocalyptic element in the later chapters of Daniel and in the Apocalypse. The lesson to do justice and love mercy was forgotten for the pleasure of setting a brand upon the Scarlet Woman,

[1] Prophetic utterances are essentially, I think, judgements of value, not of scientifically or historically established facts, although from them, from these judgements of value, we may, rightly or often alas! wrongly, deduce conclusions as to the future. To take an example: a man convinced that God is just and merciful, that these are his essential attributes, might infer, as the Prophets did, that Israel obedient or repentant will be returned to their home. He might have inferred that the Ethiopians would prevail against their invaders. But to our eyes God seems too often to be, as Napoleon said, on the side of the big battalions, of the poison gases. In the long run the Prophets may be right in some higher way, if at times we are tempted to say with Coventry Patmore:

"Great is the truth, and will prevail
When none cares whether it prevail or not."

Is not the whole of human life, all that we mean by civilisation, a long struggle to impress our values, physical and ethical, on the stubborn environment in which our life is cast, and the fundamental assumption which underlies our confused struggle, is it not the conviction that in the long run these values are invincible?

the Whore of Babylon, whether in the form of Popery or Prelacy.

But while I am prepared to admit that the prophet of things spiritual and ethical is a gifted individual and draws his inspiration from God, I am not prepared to say that it is by an entirely irrational process. I do not believe that any revelation which made no appeal to reason would carry conviction to the prophet or be communicable to his hearers. But there is a difference between reason and reasoning:

> Down Reason then, at least vain reasonings down,

says Milton in *Samson Agonistes*. Dr Saurat questions the distinction, yet I think it is a very real one. Reason is at work in many people who are quite incapable of conscious reasoning.[1] For reasoning demands at once a clear statement of premises, i.e. definitions and axioms, which few untrained people are capable of; and moreover such clear definitions are only to be got by a process of abstraction, and the result of such abstraction may be the reaching of clear but only partial truth. There are no such things in the real world as perfect circles or a purely economic man. The process of reason which I have in view is what we call "intuition". But intuition in this field—whatever it may mean when used of the pictorial arts—is not something opposed to reason. It is reason working on more subtle and complex data than the thinker can hope to define clearly. If he is to prove his conclusions he has at once to drop a great many of the premises which in the region of the half conscious, half unconscious, have been determining his own con-

[1] " The art of reasoning is not reason, often it is the abuse of reason."
Rousseau : Lettres Morales II
(Corr. Gen. III, 352)

clusions. The difference between discursive and intuitive reasoning in the field of human experience has been well described by Pascal, where he distinguishes between "l'esprit de géométrie" and "l'esprit de finesse". In the former the premisses from which we argue are clear and definite though a little remote from our everyday experience or ways of thinking, so that one has almost to turn the head a little round to one side from want of the habit. But with a very little turn one gets a full view of the premisses, and it would need a perverted mind to reason amiss on premisses so broad that it is almost impossible for them to escape attention. But with "l'esprit de finesse" (which I will call "intuition" or one kind of intuition if there be another) the premisses are well within our normal ways of thinking, are open to the eyes of the whole world. One need neither turn the head nor do oneself any violence. All one needs is to see clearly, but that one does need to do; for the premisses are so subtle, so delicate, so numerous that it is almost impossible but that some of them will escape us. Now the omission of one premiss leads to error, so that one must have a very sharp eye to take in all the principles involved and a mind capable of reasoning justly, not to reason falsely, even on well-known principles. "*Les esprits fins*", he continues, "are so accustomed to judge from a single glance that they are quite astonished when presented with propositions of which they understand nothing and to enter into which they must pass by the avenue of definition and such dry premisses that they are repelled and disgusted." There are, he adds, *esprits faux*, perverse minds, capable neither of mathematical nor of intuitive reasoning.

It is this intuitive reasoning we have in view when we say that a woman's intuition will tell her whether a man is or is not to be trusted; by which a general will see at a glance what move will save the situation. It is in this way, it seems to me, but at a greater depth, that the reason works in the prophet or the rare spirit who sees that what the world has approved hitherto is not good but evil, that what they have thought about God is not true. But this process goes on under the stress of great emotion. It is concerned not with abstract circles and squares, but with truths about his own soul and the souls of men, with questions of value. His feelings are among the premisses from which the great prophet reasons. Now the effect of a profound emotion, induced by the contemplation of a critical situation, spiritual or temporal or both, may illuminate but it may also mislead. The superior interest of tragedy to comedy is due to the fact that, faced with a crisis, the issue of which may even be death, a man not only reveals the deeper strata of his character, but himself may see deeper into the significance of his experience and of life. King Lear, on the verge of madness, yet learns from his suffering:

> Poor naked wretches, wheresoe'er you are,
> That bide the pelting of this pitiless storm,
> How shall your houseless heads and unfed sides,
> Your loop'd and window'd raggedness, defend you
> From seasons such as these? O! I have ta'en
> Too little care of this.

But Lear is speaking of and for himself, for much poetry of this intuitional kind is not prophetic in the sense I am giving to the word, because it concerns solely the individual, is spoken only to himself. A good example of this intuitional but personal feeling is Emily Brontë's:

> No coward soul is mine,
> No trembler in the world's storm-troubled sphere,
> I see Heaven's glories shine,
> And faith shines equal arming me from fear etc.

Such another is Wordsworth's *Lines Written above Tintern Abbey*. He is not saying what oft was thought, but neither is he delivering a message to men. Each of them is reading his own soul with a new depth of insight. The prophet goes further. He *has* a message, evoked by the passionate contemplation of the condition of his people, or of mankind, when faced by some profoundly disturbing crisis in their history.

If I have understood the Hebrew prophets at all, with such helps as I have had, they were faced with two things that moved them to the depth of their being, intellectual, moral and emotional. The one was the horrors of the sensual and cruel nature worship which they saw around them in neighbouring nations and among their own people. They began, or renewed, a battle which emerges ever and again, between the conception of religion as spiritual and ethical, or on the other hand as magical attempts by sacrifice, or other means, to get round the Deity. You remember the passage in Jeremiah where the prophet was told what was the complaint against his pure religion:

Then all the men which knew that their wives burned incense unto other gods, and all the women that stood by,...answered Jeremiah, saying, As for the word that thou hast spoken unto us in the name of the Lord, we will not hearken unto thee. But we will certainly perform every word that is gone forth out of our mouth, to burn incense unto the queen of heaven, and to pour out drink offerings unto her, as we have done, we and our fathers, our kings and our princes, in the cities of Judah, and in the streets of Jerusalem: for then had we plenty of victuals, and were well, and saw no evil. But since we left off to burn incense to the queen of heaven, and to pour out drink offerings unto her, we have wanted all things, and have been consumed by the sword and by the famine.[1]

And Jeremiah's reply is that it is *because* of these things that they have been driven out: "therefore this evil is happened unto you, as it is this day". Perhaps even Jeremiah was wrong; perhaps not even obedience would have saved them. But at least he has seized hold on a higher conception of religion, and one whose spread would raise men above these abominations.

The other circumstance was the political situation, the position of the people of Israel, and later of the Kingdom of Judah, between the great empires that threatened them from both sides, especially the menace of Assyria and later of Babylon. Convinced, like everyone else of every nation and of every age to almost our own day, that the final arbiter in war is the divine power, the gods, or God, Jehovah, the one and only God but also the God of Israel, there could be but one explanation of their fate, that they had gone a-whoring after other gods, the gods of nations "who have done unto their gods every abomination to Jehovah which he hateth; for even their sons and their daughters do they burn in the fire to their gods".

[1] Jeremiah xliv. 15–18.

It is from the impact of these two experiences, their conviction that God is altogether other than the gods of nature worship, is a God of justice and mercy; and the obvious peril to the existence of their people—their impact on the whole nature of the prophet, emotional, imaginative, intellectual—that all their arguments, visions and predictions flow. Of these predictions some were, and many were *not*, fulfilled, and I gather from the critics that some of the predictions which we find in our texts were later attempts to adapt what the earlier prophets had said to the actual circumstances of the return under Cyrus. I am not concerned with all this, but I would emphasise two main aspects of such prophetic, imaginative predictions. They are denunciation and promise. Jehovah is a God of righteousness and He will punish, and is punishing, the sins of the people that have gone a-whoring after strange gods, and passed their children through the fire to Moloch. "Ho Assyrian, the rod of mine anger, the staff in whose hand is mine indignation! I will send him against a profane nation, and against the people of my wrath will I give him a charge, to take the spoil, and to take the prey, and to tread them down like the mire of the streets."[1] But Jehovah is also a God of mercy and love. His heart is ever yearning over His people, open to the penitent, the sinner who returns from his sin: He will yet bring His people through their sufferings to a better time:

O Israel, return unto the Lord thy God; for thou hast fallen by thine iniquity. Take with you words, and return unto the Lord: say unto him, Take away all iniquity, and accept that

[1] Isaiah x. 5–6.

which is good: so will we render as bullocks the offering of our lips. . . . I will heal their backsliding, I will love them freely: for mine anger is turned away from him. I will be as the dew unto Israel: he shall blossom as the lily, and cast forth his roots as Lebanon. His branches shall spread, and his beauty shall be as the olive tree, and his smell as Lebanon. They that dwell under his shadow shall return; they shall revive as the corn, and blossom as the vine: the scent thereof shall be as the wine of Lebanon. Ephraim shall say, What have I to do any more with idols? . . . Who is wise, and he shall understand these things? prudent, and he shall know them? for the ways of the Lord are right, and the just shall walk in them; but transgressors shall fall therein.[1]

Sin, moral evil, as the source of all we suffer, righteousness and repentance as the promise of better things— these are the recurring themes of prophetic poetry. Take a leap for a moment to a later poem in the prophetic strain, Shelley's *Prometheus Unbound*. In his own way Shelley too is moved by the political and social condition of Europe, and he too restates the same cycle of ideas. We suffer because of our sins, in Shelley's view our want of mutual love, "man's inhumanity to man". The remedy is in our own power:

> We might be otherwise, we might be all
> We dream of, happy, high, majestical.
> Where is the love, beauty, and truth we seek
> But in our mind? and if we were not weak,
> Should we be less in deed than in desire?

And he too is confident that if we overcome we shall enjoy the same Golden Age. Now a common criticism brought against Shelley's *Prometheus Unbound* is the vagueness of the picture the poet presents, in the closing

[1] Hosea xiv. 1–9.

acts, of a regenerated world. But is Shelley more vague or more lyrical than many a passage in the books we call those of Isaiah and Jeremiah? What exactly is forecast in the eleventh chapter of Isaiah?

> And there shall come forth a shoot out of the stock of Jesse, and a branch out of his roots shall bear fruit: and the spirit of the Lord shall rest upon him, the spirit of wisdom and understanding, the spirit of counsel and might, the spirit of knowledge and of the fear of the Lord. . . .and he shall not judge after the sight of his eyes, neither reprove after the hearing of his ears: but with righteousness shall he judge the poor, and reprove with equity for the meek of the earth. . . . And the wolf shall dwell with the lamb, and the leopard shall lie down with the kid; and the calf and the young lion and the fatling together; and a little child shall lead them. . . . And the sucking child shall play on the hole of the asp, and the weaned child shall put his hand on the adder's den. They shall not hurt nor destroy in all my holy mountain: for the earth shall be full of the knowledge of the Lord, as the waters cover the sea.[1]

Christianity has given, or tried to give, a new meaning to these words which makes them refer to a still more remote future. Is anything again in Shelley (or in the passages I shall cite from Milton) more lyrical than that passage in the twenty-seventh chapter of what is generally now known as the second Isaiah?—"The spirit of the Lord God is upon me; because the Lord hath anointed me to preach good tidings unto the poor; he hath sent me to bind up the brokenhearted, to proclaim liberty to the captives, and the opening of the prison to them that are bound."[2] And Jeremiah, if it be he, is not less lyrical than Isaiah or Shelley:

[1] Isaiah xi. 1–9. "adder's" from margin.
[2] Isaiah lxi. 1–2. "the poor" from margin.

At that time, saith the Lord, will I be the God of all the families of Israel, and they shall be my people. Thus saith the Lord, The people which were left of the sword have found grace in the wilderness; even Israel, when I went to cause him to rest. The Lord appeared of old unto me, saying, Yea, I have loved thee with an everlasting love: therefore with lovingkindness have I drawn thee. Again will I build thee, and thou shalt be built, O virgin of Israel: again shalt thou be adorned with thy tabrets, and shalt go forth in the dances of them that make merry. Again shalt thou plant vineyards upon the mountains of Samaria: the planters shall plant, and shall enjoy the fruit thereof. For there shall be a day, that the watchmen upon the hills of Ephraim shall cry, Arise ye, and let us go up to Zion unto the Lord our God. For thus saith the Lord, Sing with gladness for Jacob, and shout for the chief of the nations: publish ye, praise ye, and say, O Lord, save thy people, the remnant of Israel. Behold, I will bring them from the north country, and gather them from the uttermost parts of the earth, and with them the blind and the lame, the woman with child and her that travaileth with child together: a great company shall they return hither. They shall come with weeping, and with supplications will I lead them: I will cause them to walk by rivers of waters, in a straight way wherein they shall not stumble: for I am a father to Israel, and Ephraim is my firstborn.[1]

The Hebrew is the better poet perhaps, but he is not less vague than Shelley in his vision of a regenerated mankind:

> Man, one harmonious Soul of many a soul,
> Whose nature is its own divine control,
> Where all things flow to all, as rivers to the sea;
> Familiar acts are beautiful through love;
> Labour and Pain and Grief, in life's green grove
> Sport like tame beasts, none knew how gentle they could be.
>
> His will, with all mean passions, bad delights
> And selfish cares, its trembling satellites,

[1] Jeremiah xxxi. 1–9.

A spirit ill to guide, but mighty to obey,
  Is as a tempest-wingèd ship, whose helm
  Love rules, through waves which dare not overwhelm,
Forcing life's wildest shores to own its sovereign sway.

That is the dream of the communist. A new sense of corporate life is to take the place of heaven and its harps —a dream perhaps, but is it more of a dream than that of the Hebrew prophets which was certainly not fulfilled by the return of Ezra and Nehemiah, nor is likely to be fulfilled by Lord Balfour's forcible plantation of the Jews in Arabian Palestine?[1]

But in all this the prophets were thinkers. There is reason in their reasonings even when these go astray in their immediate application. The best commentators do not fail to emphasise the warning that prophecy of the kind we meet with in the first and greatest prophets, Hosea, Isaiah, Jeremiah, has nothing in common with the utterances of what we should call psychic mediums —diviners and necromancers. The prophets speak as men possessed, but not in the sense that their own personality is pushed aside. Their inspiration is that of their whole personality, their reason is at work on premisses too manifold and profound to be brought up and defined, as science demands, without loss, without some degree of abstraction.

"People speak", says Robertson Smith, "as if the divine authority of the prophetic word were somehow dependent on, or confirmed by, the fact that the prophets enjoyed visions. That is not the doctrine of the Bible. In the New Testament St Paul lays down the principle that in true prophecy self-consciousness and self-command are never lost—the spirits of the prophets are

[1] This was written in 1937. H.J.C.G.

subject to the prophets (1 Corinthians xiv. 32). In like manner the prophets of the Old Testament never appeared before their auditors in a state of ecstasy, being thus clearly marked off from heathen soothsayers who were held to be under the influence of the godhead just in proportion as they lost intelligent self-control."

The Jewish prophets, says Duhm, committed their message to writing, which their ostensible compeers never did.

But this does not imply that they will always be able to define their thought in general terms or be able to argue logically. They will often speak in symbols, in images; for the prophet is always to a greater or less extent also a poet. All the sensuous, symbolic language of poetry can be illustrated from their writings—Allegory:

Let me sing for my wellbeloved a song of my beloved touching his vineyard. My wellbeloved had a vineyard in a very fruitful hill: and he made a trench about it, and gathered out the stones thereof, and planted it with the choicest vine, and built a tower in the midst of it, and also hewed out a winepress therein: and he looked that it should bring forth grapes, and it brought forth wild grapes. And now, O inhabitants of Jerusalem and men of Judah, judge, I pray you, betwixt me and my vineyard. What could have been done more to my vineyard, that I have not done in it? wherefore, when I looked that it should bring forth grapes, brought it forth wild grapes? And now go to; I will tell you what I will do to my vineyard: I will take away the hedge thereof, and it shall be eaten up; I will break down the fence thereof, and it shall be trodden down: and I will lay it waste; it shall not be pruned nor hoed; but there shall come up briers and thorns: I will also command the clouds that they rain no rain upon it. For the vineyard of the Lord of hosts is the house of Israel, and the men of Judah his pleasant plant: and he looked for judgement, but behold oppression; for righteousness, but behold a cry.[1]

[1] Isaiah v. 1–7.

But if the prophets are poets this does not carry with it the implication that all, but only that some, poets are prophets. Prophecy of the kind we are dealing with and poetry have their roots in the same stratum of consciousness, are a product of the same interaction of reason and feeling, the same interplay of the sub- or semi-conscious and the control of the fully conscious mind. If in the poet the fully conscious predominates, his tendency will be to didactic or declamatory reasoning in verse. If he try to subordinate the conscious control entirely he will write the gibberish which calls itself sur-realism. For if there has been and still is a disposition to look for prophecy to what Isaiah calls "them that have familiar spirits and...wizards that chirp and that mutter", in like manner there is an inclination to regard poetry as mainly a product of the sub-conscious. That is, I am convinced, a mistake. There is doubtless much that is common to poetry and dreaming, and Professor Prescott of Cornell University has written interestingly on the subject.[1] But there are also important differences. Dreams have at times not only vividness, but a surprising consistency, our reason working quite normally though on unusual premises. But we cannot count on the duration of such dreams and we cannot compel them either to stay or to return at our bidding. In a poem and in every work of art the conscious mind is finally in control. The poem may have its origin in thought and feelings that rise from the depths of the sub-conscious or semi-conscious, but any study of a poem in the process of making, e.g. the MS. of *Lycidas* or of the *Ode to*

[1] *The Poetic Mind*, by Frederick Clarke Prescott; New York, 1922.

a Nightingale, will show a constant interplay of suggestion, rejection, modification, which implies that the poet
is able to keep the mood he is expressing steadily before
his imagination as he chooses or rejects the words and
imagery and rhythm which are to express it. He can
again and again revive the mood of feeling in which the
poem took its rise, recollect the passion in tranquillity;
which does not mean that he remains tranquil in doing
so but revives the passionate mood. Wordsworth does
not mean that poetry is the expression of feeling grown
cold. Poetry is not a frigidaire. The poet is like a dyer
who, if not content with the colour he has got, can re-
steep the cloth in the dyeing vat. The poet's vat is the
mood of feeling. How different it is with dreams! Over
them we have *no* control. The best description of dreaming given us in poetry is Crabbe's *The World of Dreams*.
There you will get the impression of the evershifting
pageantry that dreams present. One enters a golden
hall of happiness, old sorrows wiped out, old quarrels
forgotten, a spirit of peace and love predominates:

> Ah me! how sweet the morning sun
>   Deigns on yon sleepy town to shine!
> How soft those far-off rivers run—
>   Those trees their leafy heads decline;
> Balm-breathing zephyrs, all divine,
>   Their health-imparting influence give;
> Now all that earth allows is mine—
>   Now, now I dream not, now I live.
>
> My friend, my brother lost in youth,
>   I meet in doubt and glad surprise,
> In conscious love, in fearless truth:
>   What pleasures in the meeting rise!

And then in a moment the change! Some alteration of our attitude in bed, some little disturbance in the alimentary canal, and the mood of peace and happiness is gone:

> Ah! brief enjoyment, pleasure dies
>   Even in its birth and turns to pain:
> He meets me with hard glazèd eyes!
>   He quits me, spurns me, with disdain.
>
> I sail the sea, I walk the land;
>   In all the world I am alone:
> Silent I pace the sea-worn sand,
>   Silent I view the princely throne;
> I listen heartless for the tone
>   Of winds and waters, but in vain;
> Creation dies without a groan!
>   And I without a hope remain.

And the next mood may be a sense of guilt or of danger and one labours to defend oneself but in vain. One's gun will not go off, one's sword breaks in one's hand, one's limbs will not move—and then again may come a mood of peace and happiness:

> Oh let me now possession take
>   Of this, it cannot be a dream.
> Yes now the soul must be awake—
>   These pleasures are—they do not seem.
> And is it true? O joy extreme!
>   All whom I loved and thought them dead,
> Far down in Lethe's flowing stream,
>   And with them life's best pleasures fled.

Less vivid perhaps, less illusive, the waking dream of a poem is the creation of the mind that evokes but also controls images to express a mood that it values and would keep and also communicate.

Prophets and poets—the Hebrew writers were both, and so greatly both that our religious tradition has assigned to them a place apart. But they do not stand alone. In every great literature are poets who have responded, in the same intuitive way, by the same interaction of thought, feeling and imagination, to the agitations of political and religious feeling that at times shake nations, and have clothed their thoughts in the same sensuous garb of metaphor, personification and rhythm. Such a poet in some measure was the author of *Piers Plowman*. If ever a poet wished to be a prophetic poet it was Milton, and it is to his claim that I propose to give special consideration, to ask if in his last great poems the artist and the prophet were ever quite blended. To Milton I might add Edmund Burke, whose response to the philosophy of Rousseau and the Jacobins was in the nature of prophecy, the response of his whole being rational and emotional, but never abstract and scientific. Burke is most eloquent when he is thinking most profoundly. William Blake was a prophet, but a prophet, it seems to me, led astray in some measure by a hankering after the apocalyptic. Of Wordsworth I shall speak in another chapter. Of Shelley, a difficult case, I will not attempt to say anything in the meantime.

CHAPTER II

*John Milton and the Renaissance theory of poetry—
A poem "doctrinal to a nation"—The awakening—
The "reform of reformation"*

IF ever an English poet (setting aside Blake for the
moment) deemed himself a prophet, something even
more because more expressly inspired than such a philosophical poet as he judged Spenser to be, it was Milton.
His Biblical and Classical education combined their influence to make him think of a poet as something more
than a versifier, the composer of such things as flow
"at waste from the pen of some vulgar amorist or the
trencher fury of a rhyming parasite", as one whose
work was to be justified by the lesson which the poem
inculcated. Milton's pronouncements on poetry, when
brought together from the prose works through which
they are scattered, are just those of the Italian critics
and their disciples such as Scaliger, Sidney, Ben Jonson.
The aim and end of poetry is to teach by delighting. To
achieve this the poet needs in the first place inspiration:

These abilities wheresoever they be found are the inspired gift
of God, rarely bestowed, but yet to some (though most abuse) in
every Nation: and are of power, beside the office of a pulpit, to
imbreed and cherish in a great people the seeds of virtue and public
civility, to allay the perturbations of the mind, and set the affections
in right tune, to celebrate in glorious and lofty hymns the throne
and equipage of God's almightiness, and what he works, and what
he suffers to be wrought with high providence in his Church, to
sing the victorious agonies of Martyrs and Saints, the deeds and

triumphs of just and pious nations doing valiantly through faith against the enemies of Christ, to deplore the general relapses of Kingdoms and States from justice and God's true worship. Lastly, whatsoever in religion is holy and sublime, in virtue amiable or grave, whatsoever hath passion or admiration in the changes of that which is called fortune from without, or the wily suttleties and refluxes of man's thoughts from within, all these things with a solid and treatable smoothness to paint out and describe.

With inspiration must go character and learning. The good poet will, as Quintilian judges of the orator, be a good man:

"for doubtless that indeed according to art is most eloquent which returns and approaches nearest to nature from whence it came, and they express nature best who in their lives least wander from her safe leading, which may be called regenerate reason. So that how he should be truly eloquent who is not withall a good man, I see not." "And long it was not after when I was confirmed in this opinion, that he who would not be frustrate of his hope to write well hereafter in laudable things, ought himself to be a true poem, that is a composition and pattern of the best and honourablest things; not presuming to sing high praises of heroic men or famous cities unless he have in himself the experience and the practice of all that which is praiseworthy."

Character; but also learning. The Renaissance had no illusions about the vernal wood taking the place of the University: "to this must be added industrious and select reading, steady observation, insight into all seemly and generous arts and affairs." And the poet must have art. Shakespeare wanted art, said Jonson, and Milton means much the same thing when he speaks of him as

Warbling his native woodnotes wild,

and contrasts his easy numbers with "the slow en-
deavouring art" of such a poet as Jonson. And by "art"
Milton and Jonson meant the same thing:

> That sublime art which in Aristotle's *Poetics*, in Horace, and
> the Italian commentaries of Castelvetro, Tasso, Mazzoni, and
> others teaches what the laws are of a true epic poem, what
> of a dramatic, what of a lyric, what decorum is, which is the
> grand master to observe. This would make them [the scholars in
> Milton's ideal school] soon perceive what despicable creatures
> our common rimers and playwrights be, and shew them what
> religious, what glorious and magnificent use might be made of
> poetry both in divine and human things.

In all this Milton is only saying in his own impassioned
manner what Sidney and Ben Jonson had said before
him, and what was in Spenser's mind when he sat down
to compose his great poem which also was to be "doctrinal to a nation". It was the experience through which
Milton was to pass that made his conception of the
poetry he wished to write more prophetic in tone than
Spenser's, that made the idea of inspiration more and
more central to his conception of poetry, and indeed
ultimately of his own life:

> Descend from Heav'n Urania, by that name
> If rightly thou art call'd, whose voice divine
> Following, above the Olympian Hill I soar,
> Above the flight of Pegasean wing.
> The meaning, not the name I call: for thou
> Nor of the Muses nine, nor on the top
> Of old Olympus dwell'st, but Heavenly borne,
> Before the Hills appear'd, or Fountain flow'd,
> Thou with Eternal wisdom didst converse,
> Wisdom thy sister, and with her didst play

> In presence of the Almighty Father, pleas'd
> With thy Celestial Song. . . .
>
>   Still govern thou my Song,
> Urania, and fit audience find though few,
> But drive far off the barbarous dissonance
> Of Bacchus and his revellers, the Race
> Of that wild Rout that tore the Thracian Bard
> In Rhodope, where Woods and Rocks had ears
> To rapture, till the savage clamour drown'd
> Both harp and voice; nor could the Muse defend
> Her son. So fail not thou, who thee implores:
> For thou art heav'nly, she an empty dream.

"And indeed, from my youth up I have been fired with zeal which kept urging me, if not to do great deeds myself, at least to celebrate them" (*Defensio Prima*).

Thus it was that Milton had thought of poetry from the age of nineteen when he composed the lines *For a Vacation Exercise*:

> Yet I had rather if I were to choose
> Thy service in some greater subject use,

and he found the sanction for this exalted view alike in the Bible, in the great Greek and Latin authors, and in the tradition of classical criticism. So, when Milton went down from Cambridge, refused or refusing a fellowship (I know not which), and when he made it clear to his indulgent father that it was his intention to follow no recognised profession, but to devote himself to poetry, we must not think of him as of a young man to-day choosing a literary career, but rather think of him as one who, rightly or wrongly, believed himself to be preparing for a high and sacred calling, to be the author of "an elaborate song to generations", a poem "doctrinal to a nation".

I do not propose to review at length the preparation for this end, the days at Horton with occasional visits to London, the years during which he acquired the extensive learning which he like other poets of the Renaissance thought essential for the serious poet, nor recall how unwillingly he turned aside at the call of *pietas* to write the magnificent elegy, that touchstone of poetic taste which is *Lycidas*:

> Yet once more, O ye laurels, and once more
> Ye myrtles brown, with ivy never sere,
> I come to pluck your berries harsh and crude,
> And with forced fingers rude,
> Shatter your leaves before the mellowing year.

With this intention in mind he visited Italy and interchanged Latin verses with his friends in the academies of Florence. To the Marquis of Manso in Naples he gave the fullest adumbration of his purpose; and on his return, as we learn from the *Epitaphium Damonis*, he made his first essay, but found himself not yet master of his theme or medium.

It is one thing to cherish a purpose, born, in part of one's consciousness of possessing more than ordinary powers, in part of the critical theory of the day, to write a didactic poem. It is another to be touched with the fire that makes one for good or ill, against or with one's will, a prophet, burdened with a message which is to be delivered, cost what it may:

This is that which the sad prophet Jeremiah laments, "Woe is

me, my mother, that thou hast borne me a man of strife and
contention." And although divine inspiration must certainly
have been sweet to those ancient prophets, yet the irksomeness of
that truth which they brought was so unpleasant to them that
everywhere they call it a burden. Yea, that mysterious book of
Revelation which the great Evangelist was bid to eat, as it had
been some eye-brightening electuary of knowledge and foresight,
though it were sweet in his mouth and in the learning, it was
bitter in his belly; bitter in the denouncing. . . . But when God
commands to take the trumpet and blow a dolorous or a jarring
blast, it lies not in man's will what he shall say or what he shall
conceal. If he shall think to be silent, as Jeremiah did, because of
the reproach and derision he met with daily, and all his familiar
friends watcht for his halting to be revenged on him for speaking
the truth, he would be forc't to confess as he confest, his word
was in my heart as a burning fire shut up in my bones, I was
weary with forbearing and could not stay, which might teach
these times not suddenly to condemn all things that are sharply
spoken, or vehemently written, as proceeding out of stomach,
virulence and ill-nature. *The Reason of Church Government.
The Second Book.*

These are Milton's own words, and one must take them
seriously if one is to understand the Man and his Work
aright, whatever view one may come to in the end regarding Milton's claim to be a prophet or the worth
of his message. The meeting of the Long Parliament
and the vista which seemed to open before him in
the months that followed his return to England, of
reform in Church and State, did affect Milton profoundly, did seem to lay on him a burden to be borne,
even at the cost of laying aside the plans he was meditating for a great poem, and did ultimately change his
conception of what that poem was to be. I cannot,

therefore, agree with Mr Belloc, writing on the great heretic Milton, that the first prelatical tracts mark no new experience, no awakening in Milton. The actual controversy regarding Bishops and Presbyters may be uninteresting to us, and Milton himself was soon to discover that

New Presbyter is but Old Priest writ large:

nor is the controversy well managed by Milton. It is more clearly and effectively conducted by Robert, Lord Brooke (cousin and heir to the Elizabethan poet and biographer of Sidney) in the Discourse Opening that Episcopacie which is Exercised in England, issued in the November of the year in which Milton's first three pamphlets appeared, 1641. It is not Milton's argument which is of importance, but the spirit and style in which he wrote. Can any candid person read such passages as that already cited, or such as I shall now cite, and not feel that they are the words of one stirred to the depth of his soul? Can he read them, whether he approve or not, without sympathy, without some degree of compassion and foreboding? It is dangerous to hope so ardently for any great and sudden amelioration in the lot of man, for such high hopes seldom outlive the first days of a revolution, as we have seen too often since Milton's day, in revolutions French, Turkish, Russian, German, Spanish —one short day of hope and mutual goodwill to be followed by disillusionment, mutual suspicion and hatred, and a grim roll of executions. Milton writes in a mood of such exaltation as Wordsworth when he felt that:

> Bliss was it in that dawn to be alive,
> But to be young was very heaven.

"Now once again by all concurrence of signs, and by the general instinct of holy and devout men, as they daily and solemnly express their thoughts, God is decreeing to begin some new and great period in his Church, even to the reforming of reformation itself; what does he then but reveal himself to his servants, and as his manner is, first to his Englishmen!"[1] "Then amidst the hymns and halleuiahs of saints someone may be heard offering at high strains in new and lofty measures, to sing and celebrate thy divine mercies and marvellous judgements in this land throughout all ages; whereby this great and warlike nation instructed and inured to the fervent and continual practice of Truth and Righteousness, and casting far from her the rags of her old vices, may press on hard to that high and happy emulation to be found the soberest, wisest, and most Christian People, at that day when thou the Eternal and shortly expected King shalt open the clouds to judge the several kingdoms of the world, and distributing national honours and rewards to religious and just common-wealths, shalt put an end to all earthly tyrannies, proclaiming thy universal and mild monarchy through Heaven and Earth; where they undoubtedly that by their labours counsels and prayers have been earnest for the common good of religion and their country shall receive, above the inferior orders of the blessed, the regal addition of Principalities, Legions and Thrones into their glorious titles, and in supereminence of beatific vision progressing the dateless and irrevoluble circle of Eternity shall clasp inseparable hands with joy and bliss in over measure for ever."[2]

Even in that thorny and repellent pamphlet, the *Animadversions upon the Remonstrant's Defence against Smectymnuus*, Milton turns aside to write in the same prophetic, or rather apocalyptic, strain:

[1] *Areopagitica.*   [2] *Of Reformation.*

Let us all go every true protested Briton throughout the three kingdoms, and render thanks to God the Father of Light and fountain of heavenly grace, and to His son Christ our Lord; leaving this remonstrant and his adherents to their own designs, and let us recount even here without delay the patience and long-suffering that God hath us'd towards our blindness and hardness time after time. For he being equally near to his whole creation of Mankind, and of free power to turn his benefick and fatherly regard to what Region or Kingdom he pleases, hath yet ever had this island under the special indulgent eye of his Providence.

And after a reference to Wycklif and the earlier reform in England Milton goes on:

O if we freeze at noon after their early thaw, let us fear lest the sun for ever hide himself, and turn his orient steps from our ingrateful Horizon, justly condemned to be eternally benighted. Which dreadful judgement, O thou the ever-begotten Light, and perfect Image of thy Father, intercede, may never come upon us, as we trust thou hast.... Thou hast discovered the plots, and frustrated the hopes of all the wicked in the Land; and put to shame the persecutors of thy Church: thou hast made our false prophets to be found a lie in the sight of all the people, and chas'd them with sudden confusion and amazement before the redoubled brightness of thy descending cloud that now covers thy Tabernacle. Who is there that cannot trace thee now in thy beamy walk through the midst of thy sanctuary, amidst those golden candlesticks which have long suffered a dimness amongst us through the violence of those that had seiz'd them, and were more taken with the mention of their gold than of their starry light; teaching the doctrine of Balaam to cast a stumbling-block before thy servants, commanding them to eat things sacrific'd to idols and forcing them to fornication? Come therefore, O thou that hast the seven stars in thy right hand, appoint the chosen priests according to their orders and courses of old, to minister before thee, and duly to press and pour out the consecrated oil into thy holy and ever-burning lamps.... O perfect and accomplish thy glorious acts; for men may leave their works unfinish'd, but thou art a God, thy nature is perfection; shouldst thou bring us thus far onwards from Egypt to destroy us in this wilderness though *we* deserve, yet thy great name would suffer in the rejoicing of thine enemies, and the deluded hopes of all thy servants. When thou hast settled peace in the Church and righteous judgement in the Kingdom then shall all thy saints address their voices of joy and triumph to thee, standing on the shore of that Red Sea into which our enemies had almost driven us. And he that now for haste snatches up a plain ungarnish'd present as a thank-offering to thee which could not be deferr'd in regard of thy so many late deliverances wrought for us one upon another, may then perhaps take up a harp and sing thee an elaborate Song to Generations.... Come forth out of thy royal chambers, O Prince of all the Kings of the earth, put on the visible robes of thy imperial majesty, take up that unlimited sceptre which thy Almighty father hath bequeathed thee; for now the voice of thy Bride calls thee, and all creatures sigh to be renewed.

Does that differ very much in tone from the spirit and tone of such an expostulation as the following from the sixty-third chapter of Isaiah (lxiii. 15 to lxiv end):—

Look down from heaven, and behold from the habitation of thy holiness and of thy glory: where is thy zeal and thy mighty acts? the yearning of thy bowels and thy compassions are restrained toward me. For thou art our father, though Abraham knoweth us not, and Israel doth not acknowledge us: thou, O Lord, art our father; our redeemer from everlasting is thy name. O Lord, why dost thou make us to err from thy ways, and hardenest our heart from thy fear? Return for thy servants' sake, the tribes of thine inheritance. Thy holy people possessed it but a little while: our adversaries have trodden down thy sanctuary. We are become as they over whom thou never barest rule; as they that were not called by thy name. Oh that thou wouldest rend the heavens, that thou wouldest come down, that the mountains might quake at thy presence.... When thou didst terrible things which we looked not for, thou camest down, the mountains flowed down at thy presence. For from of old men have not heard, nor perceived by the ear, neither hath the eye seen a God beside thee, which worketh for him that waiteth for him. Thou sparest him that rejoiceth and worketh righteousness, those that remember thee in thy ways: behold, thou wast wroth, and we sinned.... For we are all become as one that is unclean, and all our righteousnesses are as a polluted garment: and we all do fade as a leaf; and our iniquities, like the wind, take us away.... But now, O Lord, thou art our father; we are the clay, and thou our potter; and we all are the work of thy hand. Be not wroth very sore, O Lord, neither remember iniquity for ever: behold, look, we beseech thee, we are all thy people. Thy holy cities are become a wilderness, Zion is become a wilderness, Jerusalem a desolation. Our holy and our beautiful house, where our fathers praised thee, is burned with fire; and all our pleasant things are laid waste. Wilt thou refrain thyself for these things, O Lord? wilt thou hold thy peace, and afflict us very sore?

Were it not for the beauty of Milton's prose it would be easier to say that his words were those of one temporarily exalted beyond the limits of complete sanity—"Paul, thou art mad; thy much learning doth turn thee to madness"—than the words of one who has undergone no disturbing experience. Indeed, to understand the next and more disastrous experience, that of his marriage, one must realise the high-strung nature of the man and the frame of mind in which he was when that blow fell.

Nor without realising this can we do justice to Milton's style in these pamphlets. Others write more persuasively than Milton. They write as controversialists, he as a prophet. Milton's prose presents a double

aspect. It is the prose of one who had formed his idea
of good prose from Latin oratory, and is an instructive
comment on the doctrine that used to be current as
to the beneficial effect of Latin composition on one's
English prose. How little English Milton had written
before 1641! Even for letters to his friends he had
used Latin, as was the custom of the Humanists.
Nothing proved harder than to adapt the Latin period
to English. It could be done better in verse than in prose.
Compare the excellent period with which Chaucer opens
the *Prologue* to the *Canterbury Tales* with his attempts to
carry over into English the periods of Boethius; nay,
compare the periods in *Paradise Lost* with many in
Milton's prose. The faults of Milton's periods are,
Saintsbury says, temperamental—due that is to the
poetic, prophetic strain of which I am speaking. They
are due in the second place, he continues, to the "extraordinary fullness of mind which led him to cram his
sentences with quotations, argument, parenthesis, and
every figured and unfigured trick of eking and bolstering
out sentence and paragraph". "The most serious fault
is his habit of joining on relative and epexegetical
clauses at the last, some statement, some after-thought
which thus brought in weakens the sonority, the
triumphant close of an oratorical period." For Milton's
prose is the prose of an orator who has also the imagination, the gift of beautiful, felicitous, poignant imagery of
a poet, and the exalted mood of a self-confident prophet.
Milton's pamphlets are not to be read as of quite the
same kind as those of many fellow-pamphleteers on
either side. Professor Haller of Columbia University

has done good service by bringing together a number of
tracts illustrative of the defence of toleration and its
developement into a democratic demand for freedom in
the State and in trade, the levelling doctrines on which
Cromwell ultimately had to put down his foot. Many of
them are written in a clearer, more persuasive, more
practical style than Milton's, some of them in a finer
temper, for Milton's prophetic vehemence has somewhat of the temper of a fanatic like John Lilburne, if on
the other hand his liberal spirit links him with such
finer spirits as John Goodwin, William Walwyn, Henry
Robinson and Richard Overton. He differs from both
groups by the exalted, prophetic tone of one whose
vision goes far beyond the demands of the moment.

It is as a prophet, then, one burdened with a message
which it is laid on him to deliver, that Milton writes in
these first contributions to the religious and political
warfare of the day; and it is only by considering them as
such prophetic outcries that one can do justice to their
strange contrasts, passages of angry argument and
invective on the one hand and lofty prophetic and apocalyptic flights on the other. I would therefore take at
their face value Milton's disclaimers of personal malevolence, his affirmation and reaffirmation of the burden
which he feels laid upon him:

"And therefore they that love the souls of men, which is the
dearest love, and stirs up the noblest jealousy, when they meet with
such collusion, cannot be blamed though they be transported with
the zeal of truth to a well-heated fervency; especially seeing they
which thus offend against the souls of their brethren do it with
delight to their great gain, ease, and advancement in this world; but

they that seek to discover and oppose their false trade of deceiving do it not without a sad and unwilling anger, not without many hazards; but without all private and personal spleen, and without any thought of earthly reward, when as this very course they take stops their hope of ascending above a lowly and unenviable pitch in this life."[1] "But when God commands to take the trumpet and blow a dolorous or jarring blast it lies not in man's will what he shall say, or what he shall conceal."[2]

Nothing could be much worse than the temper and the manner in which Milton assails Bishop Hall in the *Animadversions*. Yet in the very midst of coarse abuse and clumsy humour emerges the exalted invocation from which I have already quoted, and the vindication of the Present Age. It is to me difficult to read such an outburst and to refuse to give Milton full credit—whatever one may think of his wisdom—when he declares that his anger is not personal but an anger of the spirit. Yet it is undoubtedly difficult to recover the mind and temper of an age and an individual, when a great poet could gloat as Milton does over the doom that awaits the bishops in another world:

But they contrary that by the impairing and diminution of the true Faith, the distresses and servitude of their country, aspire to high dignity, rule and promotion here, after a shamefull end in this life (which God grant them) shall be thrown down eternally into the darkest and deepest Gulf of Hell, where under the despightful controul, the trample and spurn of all the other damned, that in the anguish of their torture shall have no other ease than to exercise a ravening and bestial tyranny over them as their slaves and negro's, they shall remain in that plight for ever, the basest, the lowermost, the most dejected, most underfoot and downtrodden Vassals of Perdition.

[1] *Animadversions.*   [2] *The Reason of Church Government.*

If there is any literary model for such an outburst it must be sought, I suspect, in the *Divina Commedia*, for Dante too has no scruples about committing personal and political foes to eternal torment.

But it remains to ask what are the grounds of his fears and hopes, what is the central conviction from which Milton reasons whether intuitively or in a more ratiocinative manner? We have seen what is the conviction from which the Hebrew prophets draw their intuitive inferences of impending doom or ultimate restoration. It is their new and overpowering conviction of the righteousness of God, that the God of Israel, of the Jews, is the God of the whole earth, a God of righteousness and mercy, not to be seduced by rites and sacrifices, least of all by passing one's own children through the fire, but only by doing justice and loving mercy and walking humbly with Him. From what conviction or convictions, religious and ethical, does Milton start in his denunciation of Antichrist in the form of popery or prelacy?

I have no intention of claiming for Milton that he was a prophet to whom were revealed new and unfamiliar but powerful and on reflection convincing truths. He is not a prophet in the sense in which prophetic inspiration is claimed for at least the greatest of the Hebrew prophets, in the sense in which the centre of Christian worship is both the last and the greatest of the Hebrew prophets. Of course also I do not know, if anyone does, the extent to which the Hebrew prophets' thought had been prepared for before they became its mouthpiece. But Milton's inspiration came from the spirit that had been moving over the waters of European religious thought for more than a century and was at work in those around him. It is as a Protestant and Puritan in the first place that Milton speaks, and I must try to make clear to myself the essential element—*das Wesen*—of the Protestant movement. Such a study as Pontien Polman's *L'Élément Historique dans la Controverse religieuse du XVIᵉ Siècle* (1932) makes it clear that none of the greater Reformers, in their appeal to the Bible, intended to ignore altogether the history of the Church, or to overlook the importance of the Fathers and the early Councils, as guides in the interpretation of the Bible. The contention alike of Luther, of Melanchthon, and of Calvin is that they are restoring the purity and simplicity of the early Church. It was a difficult position to maintain, and Milton, very early in the course of the controversy over episcopacy, grows contemptuous of "Antiquarians" and from all citation of Fathers and Councils makes appeal direct to the Bible. On that basis he is in the end to build the whole scheme of theology and ethics which he expounds so clearly in the *De Doctrina* of his later years:

"Let them chant while they will of prerogatives, we shall tell them of Scripture; of custom, we of Scripture; of Acts and Statutes, still of Scripture, till the quick and piercing word enter to the dividing of their souls and the mighty weakness of the Gospel throw down the weak mightiness of man's reasoning." "But I trust they for whom God has reserved the honour of reforming this Church will easily perceive their adversary's drift in this calling for antiquity: they fear the plain field of the Scriptures; the chase is too hot; they seek the dark, the bushy, the tangled forest, they would imbosk; they feel themselves strook in the transparent streams of divine truth; they would plunge and tumble, and think to lie hid in the foul weeds and muddy water, where no plummet can reach the bottom. But let them beat themselves like whales, and spend their oil till they be dredg'd ashore: though wherefore should the ministers give them so much line for shifts and delays? Wherefore should they not urge only the Gospel, and hold it ever in their faces like a mirror of diamond till it dazzle and pierce their misty eyeballs? Maintaining it the honour of its absolute sufficiency and supremacy inviolable: for if the Scripture be for reformation and antiquity to boot, it is but an advantage to the dozen, it is no winning cast; and though antiquity be against it while the Scriptures be for it, the cause is as good as ought to be wished, antiquity itself sitting judge."[1]

But what was the emotional background to this zealous and contentious study of Scripture and the Fathers? It is difficult to-day to do justice to the Protestant Reformation, so strongly has the tide turned against it in the minds of the young even in Scotland. Of Protestantism and Puritanism one may almost say: "There's none so poor to do them reverence." Yet there was something in the movement that seemed to many of enormous importance if human passions exaggerated distinctions and darkened counsel; and Puritanism was just the Protestantism of the Protestant religion, and Milton represents the very essence of Puritanism. That essential was, it seems to me, the ever recurring conflict between the ethical in religion and the magical. Rightly or wrongly many men had come to see in Catholic worship, in the central doctrine of the Mass and all the beliefs and practices that had developed about it, and in the reverence of the Virgin and the Saints, in images and relics and indulgences, to see and to feel about these things very much as the Hebrew prophets

[1] *Of Reformation.*

had felt about oblations and incense and new moons
and appointed feasts, and the sacrifice of bullocks or the
passing of one's children through the fire to Moloch.[1]
Jeremiah, if I follow Professor Welch, was opposed not
only to the burning of incense to the Queen of Heaven
and pouring out drink offerings to her, but to the re-
forms and the Temple worship of Josiah. These were
all magical attempts to secure the favour of God, de-
vices for getting into Heaven despite one's sins. That
there was much more than this in mediaeval Catholicism
I need not, of course, say. It was proved by the strength
of the Catholic Counter-Reformation. I am not concerned to justify Protestant feeling, but simply with the
fact that many people did so feel, honestly I believe and
not, as Mr Belloc and some others would suggest, by
inspiration of the Devil.

Right or wrong this is the central, the dominant thought
of Milton in these early pamphlets. The influence of
this thought, combined with his belief in the reason as
our supreme guide, led Milton from position to position till in the end he stood alone, outside all visible
churches, so that he dedicates his *De Doctrina* as John
Milton to all the Churches. The spiritual for him must
be kept pure of all carnal, material, magical pollution:

Sad it is to think how that doctrine of the gospel, planted by
teachers divinely inspired, and by them winnowed and sifted from
the chaff of overdated ceremonies, and refined to such a spiritual
height and temper of purity, and knowledge of the Creator, that
the body, with all the circumstances of time and place, were

[1] And the Inquisition appeared to many to be engaged in a very
similar manner, passing their children through the fire to avert the anger
of God.

purified by the affections of the regenerate soul and nothing left impure, but sin; Faith needing not the weak and fallible office of the senses, to be either the ushers or interpreters of heavenly mysteries, save where our Lord himself in his sacraments ordained; that such a doctrine should. . .drag so downwards as to backslide into the Jewish beggary of old cast rudiments, and stumble forward another way into the new-vomited paganism of sensual idolatry, attributing purity or impurity to things indifferent, that they might bring the inward acts of the spirits to the outward and customary eye-service of the body. . . . Then was baptism changed into a kind of exorcism, and water sanctified by Christ's institute thought little enough to wash off the original spot without the scratch or cross impression of a priest's forefinger...even that feast of love and heavenly admitted fellowship, the seal of filial grace, became the subject of horror and glouting adoration pageanted about like a dreadful idol. (*Of Reformation.*)

But the finest, the most dignified passage (and there are not many of calm dignity in the stormy and occasionally exalted prose of Milton) is in *The Reason of Church Government etc.*, Milton's plea for the purely spiritual character of Church discipline as contrasted with the Civil discipline which begins and ends in the body. The State was not concerned to change men's minds but simply to prevent them from doing certain things or punish them for doing them. It was for the Church—and Milton is speaking at the time as a Presbyterian—to discipline the mind and soul of man, and her instruments are purely of the spirit—Instruction, Admonition, Reproof, and finally Excommunication, the door being always kept open for repentance. The Church's sanctions are not, or ought not to be, fines and imprisonment and pillories and cutting off of ears. The Church's sanction is *aidos*:

"shame, or to call it better the reverence of our elders, our brethren, our friends. . . . And certain it is that whereas terror is thought such a great stickler in a Commonwealth, honourable shame is a far greater, and has more reason. For where shame is there is fear, but where fear is there is not presently shame.". . .
. . . "But there is yet a more ingenuous and noble degree of honest shame, or call it if you will an esteem whereby men bear an inward reverence toward their own persons. And if the love of God, as a fire sent from Heaven, to be ever kept alive upon the altar of our hearts, be the first principle of all godly and vertuous actions in men, this pious and just honouring of ourselves is the second, and may be thought as the radical moisture and fountainhead whence every laudable and worthy enterprise issues forth. And although I have given it the name of a liquid thing, yet is it not incontinent to bound itself, as humid things are, but hath in it a most restraining and powerful abstinence to start back, and globe itself upwards from the mixture of any ungenerous and unbeseeming motion, or any soil wherewith it may peril to stain itself. Something, I confess, it is to be ashamed of evil doing in the presence of any; and to reverence the opinion and the countenance of a good man rather than a bad, fearing most in his sight to offend, goes so far as almost to be vertuous; yet this is still but the fear of infamy, and many such when they find themselves alone, saving their reputation will compound with other scruples, but come to a close treaty with their dearer vices in secret. But he that holds himself in reverence and due esteem, both for the dignity of God's image upon him and for the price of his redemption, which he thinks is visibly marked upon his forehead, accounts himself a fit person to do the noblest and godliest deeds, and much better worth than to deject and defile with such a debasement and pollution as sin is, himself so highly ransomed and ennobled to a new friendship and filial relation with God. Nor can he fear so much the offence and reproach of others as he dreads and would blush at the reflection of his own severe and modest eye upon himself if it should see him doing or imagining that which is sinful though in the deepest secrecy."

To secure this high temper Milton thinks there is no
better way than to make a man feel

that as he is called by the high calling of God to be holy and
pure so is he by the same appointment ordained and by the
Churches' call admitted to such offices of discipline in the Church
to which his own spiritual gifts by the example of Apostolic in-
stitution have autoriz'd him. For we have learnd that the scornful
term of laic, the consecrating of Temples, carpets and table-cloths,
the railing in of a repugnant and contradictive Mount Sinai in the
Gospel, as if the touch of a lay Christian who is never the less
God's living temple could profane dead Judaisms, the exclusion
of Christ's people from the offices of holy discipline through the
pride of a usurping clergy, causes the rest to have an unworthy and
abject opinion of themselves; to approach the holy duties with a
slavish fear and to unholy doings with a familiar boldness. For
seeing such a wide and terrible distance between religious things
and themselves, and that in respect of a wooden table and the
perimeter of holy ground about it, a flagon pot and a linen
corporal, the Priest esteems their layships unhallow'd and unclean,
they fear religion with such a fear as loves not and think the
purity of the Gospell too pure for them.

This then is Milton the Puritan (and in these years
a Presbyterian), a Puritan who will find holiness in
nothing material, in nothing but the soul of man regenerated by the Grace of God[1]—no holy buildings, or
altars, or tables, or pots, or copes—nor yet Holy Orders
—and this last refusal will bring him, when the impulse
comes from a personal injury, out of the Presbyterian

---

[1] The Mount of Paradise is swept away by the Flood and left:
"an island salt and bare,
The haunt of seals, and orcs, and sea-mews' clang,
To teach thee that God attributes to place
No sanctity, if none be thither brought
By men who there frequent, or therein dwell." *P.L.* xi. 834 ff.

fold, to fight an ever lonelier battle in which his captain
will be his own reason interpreting the word of Scripture. Milton is always both Humanist and Protestant
—Protestant in his respect for the Bible, Humanist in
his confidence in his own reason as the interpreter of the
Bible, in his conviction that reason is the supreme gift of
God to men, God's own image in Man, a gift obscured
by sin, by the Fall, but regenerate in the Christian.

In these early pamphlets we are in touch also with the
Milton who is contemplating a great poem on a national
theme. Taking as evidence those of the passages I have
cited which concern what is to be his own part in the
great regeneration of England to which Parliament is
to lead the way, his work is to be a poem, historical in
theme, symbolic in some way or other of the awakening
experience through which England is again passing—
perhaps still an *Arthuriad*, though how Milton the
Puritan would have dealt with the central episodes of
Lancelot and Guinevere, and the high history of the
Holy Grail, is hard to conjecture. The list of subjects set
out in the manuscript in Trinity College and the sketches
of drama there are not to be taken as proof that he had
abandoned either the epic form or the historical subject.
They represent, it may be, his first reactions from the
failure referred to in the *Epitaphium Damonis*, or, it may
be, various *parerga* with which he might busy himself till
he saw more clearly the course of events and the most
fitting way in which to celebrate the new age. It was not
till he had written the *Defensio Secunda* (1654) that the
idea of a national historical poem was abandoned, as being
in a way completed—but of that later.

CHAPTER III

The first shock—Marriage and divorce—A pause in pamphleteering and return to poetry—The first decisive step—Regicide

BUT before any such poem was more than a dream, part of the larger dream of a "reform of Reformation", a regenerate England in which not only had Prelacy disappeared but the Parliament should have taken in hand the right ordering of men's lives from the education of children to "the management of our public sports and festival pastimes", came the shock of Milton's marriage and his desertion by his wife. I need not resume the history, largely conjectural, of Milton's marriage, the causes that led to it, or the experiences which ensued for wife and husband. The redating of his departure from London and return as a married man has put events in a better perspective if it has not dispelled all mystery. But my concern is with the effect this shock, and the reception of the pamphlets called forth by the experience, i.e. Milton's treatises on divorce (which he afterwards regretted he had not written in Latin), had upon what I am calling the prophet in Milton, his consciousness of a message which it was laid on him to deliver. In the prelatical pamphlets he had written as the champion of a cause, a prophet who knew that he spoke for others as well as for himself. In undertaking to restate the doctrine and discipline of divorce he may have thought that he was defending the same cause of Christian liberty in another field, and looked for support to at least many in the same Presbyterian fold. One gathers that from the appeal he makes, when opposition arises, to the leading Reformers—Bucer, Fagius, Grotius. Milton soon discovered his error; and his marriage, with the controversy it led to, had a double consequence: firstly, the shock to the sensitive, emotional temperament of which the passages I have cited are evidence, and secondly, the breach which the pamphlets precipitated between himself and those with whom he had entered the battle; the beginning of Milton's isolation, his quest of other allies, his movement more and more towards what we might call "the left", the Independents, the Army and its leaders, a movement which is to lead him from one disillusion to another until at the Restoration he sits alone, allied to no church and no party, disillusioned but undiscouraged and unrepentant and ready in his poems to put on record his reading of man's character and history.

Of Milton's conclusions regarding marriage and divorce I should like to say a few words, but I shall not attempt to discuss his rather desperate efforts to harmonise the words of Christ with the Mosaic legislation. To Mr Belloc these pamphlets seem the worst thing Milton ever wrote, an assault upon the sacredness and indissoluble nature of marriage as felt throughout the Christian and Catholic Middle Ages. That marriage was a sacrament and indissoluble was the theory of the Catholic Church. That however the sacredness of marriage was deeply and widely felt is, I confess, hard to realise by anyone who has read much of mediaeval literature, courtly, popular, or devout. For the religious idealisation of Virginity was itself somewhat of a slur on marriage. The first Christian pronouncement on marriage, after the great words of Christ "which cost Milton all that pain", is St Paul's "It is better to marry than to burn"; not a very elevated doctrine, but the words express the spirit of much that the Fathers of the Church had to say on the subject. Nor does one get an exalted conception of marriage from the love-poetry of the Middle Ages, courtly and romantic or popular and realistic, nor from the literature of comedy in which cuckoldry plays so prominent a part. It was, as I have argued elsewhere, the growing reverence for the marriage tie which the Reformation brought with it that forced to the front the question of the dissolubility of marriage.

That is clear from Milton's pamphlets. The motive which inspired his championship of divorce was not the usual one, that he had fallen in love with another woman. He was no Shelley, ready to take wing towards each new flame that dazzled him, to seek a fresh soul's-mate, and convinced that

> True love in this differs from gold and clay
> That to divide is not to take away,

though Milton too was to become a defender in theory of polygamy. The motive which animated his passionate longing for escape from the bond he had too rashly taken upon himself was the absolute want of response in the woman he had married, not physical response (there is no evidence that she refused to consummate the marriage), but an entire and unconcealed want of sympathy, of any understanding of his mind and heart. He had dreamed so highly of love and marriage and he had "made himself the bondman of a luckless and helpless matrimony", met with "a mute and spiritless mate". Nothing could be more passionate than the language in which Milton refers to what had been his own experience. What of the cheerfulness becoming a Christian is to be expected of one "in such a bosom affliction as this, crushing the very foundation of his inmost nature, when he shall be forced to love against a possibility, and to use a dissimulation against his own soul in the perpetual and ceaseless duties of a husband"? It is "to cover the altar of the Lord with continual tears, so that he regardeth not the offerings any more". If we are disposed, as some readers are, to smile at these outcries, it is perhaps because we take a more experienced and cynical view of marriage than the heretic Milton. He had been one of "those persons who being of a pensive nature and course of life have summed up all their solace in that free and lightsome conversation which God and Man intends in marriage. Whereof when they see themselves deprived by meeting an unsociable consort they resent one another's mistake so deeply that long it is not ere grief end one of them." At least so it seems to Milton: "Wherein can God delight, wherein be worshipped, wherein be glorified by the forcible continuing of an improper and ill-yoking couple? He that loved not to see the disparity of several cattle at the plough, cannot be pleased with vast unmeetness in marriage." Christ "could not have meant to cut off all remedy from a good man who finds himself consuming away in a disconsolate and uninjoin'd matrimony". It is those who deem most highly of love and marriage who suffer most:

And yet there follows upon this a worse temptation: for if he be such as hath spent his youth unblamably, and laid up his chiefest earthly comforts in the enjoyment of a contented marriage, nor did neglect that furtherance which was to be obtained therein by constant prayers; when he shall find himself bound fast to an uncomplying discord of nature, or as it often happens to an image of earth and phlegm, with whom he looked to be the copartner of a sweet and gladsome society, and sees withal that his bondage is now inevitable, though he be almost the strongest Christian he will be ready to despair in virtue and mutiny against Divine Providence.

Again:

"As no man apprehends so well what vice is as he who is truly virtuous, no man knows Hell like him who converses most in Heaven; so there is none that can estimate the evil and the affliction of a natural hatred in matrimony unless he have a soul gentle enough and spacious enough to contemplate what is true love." "This pure and more inbred desire of joining to itself in conjugal fellowship a fit conversing soul (which desire is properly called love) is stronger than death, as the spouse of Christ thought, many waters cannot quench it, neither can the floods drown it."

No just reader of such passages, who will ignore the angry argument about texts from the Old and New Testaments, can fail to feel sympathy for the young, sensitive, passionate idealist and moralist who has found himself tied to "an image of earth and phlegm"—a young girl with no idea of marriage beyond having a good time—nor will he readily class Milton along with advocates of free love or easy divorce, of the claim to leave a wife with whom one has become bored for one who promises for a while to be more exciting. It is not the idealism of Catholic doctrine he is at war with so much as the realism of Catholic mediaeval practice—the combination of indissolubility in theory (which kings and great men can easily evade) and readiness to condone the "escapes", as Shakespeare would call them, which serve to lighten the burden of the yoke:

> And indeed, the papists, who are the strictest forbidders of divorce, are the easiest libertines to admit of grossest uncleanness; as if they had a design by making wedlock a supportless yoke, to violate it most, under colour of preserving it most inviolable.

That Milton's disappointment in marriage did an injury, never quite repaired, to the emotional, sympathetic side of his haughty character is, I think, undeniable. It prevented the spirit of love from penetrating the splendid but somewhat hard beauty of the later poems as that spirit does, despite of, or even in a mystical way overcoming, the horrors of the *Inferno*, and moving in an unbroken crescendo to culminate in the warmth and colour of the *Paradiso*. That the reception given to his plea for liberty in the family was also a shock, precipitating a severance which might have come in any case but more gradually, is also true. But neither the one nor the other destroyed Milton's confidence in himself, nor at once dispelled his hopes for the reforming work of Parliament. For three years his house was free from the presence of the "image of earth and phlegm". Indeed it is arguable that her return in 1646 with all her family in her train was a greater misfortune than her departure.

In the interim he wrote his *Tractate of Education* (1644) and the *Areopagitica* (1644), products of the spirit of the earlier tracts, the spirit of one who still hoped for a reform of reformation, a new Church and a new State. Again, both these tracts must be read as documents of a prophetic rather than a purely practical character. Nothing is easier than to indicate the impracticable character of Milton's scheme of education, which has more than all the faults of most schemes which ignore the fact that very few people can be educated beyond a strict limit. Yet there are one or two things to be noted in the tract. In the first place, his conception of education is comprehensive—intellectual, artistic, physical. Secondly, he is clear that Latin and Greek and other languages should be taught from the outset as instruments not as ends:

> Language is the instrument conveying to us things useful to be known. And if a linguist shall pride himself to have all the tongues that Babel cleft the world into, yet if he have not studied the solid things in them as well as the words and lexicons, he were nothing so much to be esteemed a learned man as any yeoman or tradesman competently wise in the mother dialect only.

Hence Milton's scorn for too early composition in prose and verse and his reading of Latin and Greek authors for the interest of their content: "easy and delightful books of education whereof the Greeks have store, as Cebes, Plutarch, and other Socratic discourses. But in Latin we have none." The truth of that last remark will be clear to anyone who has had to teach Latin and French. How easy to interest a pupil in French, which so soon becomes the vehicle of what is delightful to read! Whereas who can recall one thing in Latin which he read early that gave him then the slightest pleasure? Even Virgil compared with Homer was a bore, a prig, his story full of sacrifices. We cannot now of course go to Latin and Greek to study science, technical and theoretic. But it is a loss that we cannot, a loss that has weakened the claims of a classical education.

The *Areopagitica* again is not a practical treatise on that difficult problem, the limits to be set to freedom of speech. It is an impassioned, prophetic vindication of the invincibility of truth if given a fair field and no favour. Free speech is sadly at a discount to-day. The extreme wings—Catholic, Fascist, Communist—are united in distrust of the human mind left free to think, and to utter what it thinks. To those whose hope for humanity is still centred in reason Milton's tract remains a splendid prophetic hymn.

Milton was not, of course, alone in the fight for the freedom of the press. Professor Haller has selected from the mass of tracts issued between 1640 and 1649, when Cromwell suppressed the Levellers, a number illustrating the developement of the plea for religious toleration into a plea for democratic liberty in a wider range, in short for "popular representative government under a fundamental law or agreement of the people".[1] It is explicable therefore that Masson should assume that, having broken away from the dominant Presbyterian party, Milton would be found among the sectaries. To his old friends, the Smectymnuus group, Milton was now, he suggests:

[1] *Tracts on Liberty in the Puritan Revolution*, 1638–1647 ; Columbia University Press, 1934.

one of those dreadful sectaries. Nay, he was a Sectary more odious than most, for his was a moral heresy. What was Independency, what was Antinomianism, compared with the heresy of the household, the loosening of the holy relation on which all civil society depended? How detestable the doctrine that when two married people found they had made a mistake in coming together, or at least when the husband could declare before God and human witnesses his irreconcileable dissatisfaction with his wife, then it was right that the two should be separated, with liberty to each to find a new mate.

Masson goes on to imagine the kind of gossip which must have circulated "in the booksellers' shops near St Paul's and even round the Parliament in Westminster in the early months of 1644"—gossip about Milton, his Cambridge honours, his poems, his "splendid pamphlets for Church reform", about Mrs Milton, etc. etc. As a fact this is to exaggerate Milton's personal importance at this date. Haller has shown that Milton's tracts were taken comparatively little notice of. They were apparently, as perhaps might be expected, "caviare to the general". Of his personal history so little was known that:

Bishop Hall and his son, who must surely have had means of finding out whatever there was to their purpose to find out concerning their antagonist in 1642, seem to have relied upon rumour, invention and dubious inferences based upon the raciness of Milton's vocabulary.[1] Except for the replies of the Halls Milton's antiprelatical tracts went unnoticed by the press. One stigma did soon attach itself to Milton's name. *The Doctrine and Discipline of Divorce*...soon achieved a notoriety as a scandalous book. It was commonly linked with Williams's *The Bloody Tenent* (July 1644) and Richard Overton's *Man's Mortalitie* (Jan. 19, 1644).

[1] *Op. cit.* pp. 129–130.

This association was due to the fact that the three works appeared during the controversy raised by the *Apologeticall Narrative* at the opening of 1644, and that each developed what was considered a specially shocking heresy—divorce; toleration for Jews, Papists, Turks, and Pagans; the mortality of the soul.... The anonymous reply to the *Doctrine and Discipline* (Nov. 19) does show acquaintance with Milton's book, but none with Milton himself, a striking lack since the author would certainly have had no scruple in making use of any knowledge he had of Milton's marital unhappiness—

and the desertion of his wife, had he known of it. One has only to recall Milton's own treatment of Salmasius and his shrewish wife. Milton was dubbed a "divorcer" by writers who knew little or nothing of his work, and no reasoned reply was forthcoming such as he asks for at the end of *Colasterion*:

If his intents be sincere to the public, and shall carry him on without bitterness to the opinion, or to the person dissenting; let him not, I intreat him, guess by the handling, which meritoriously hath been bestowed on this object of contempt and laughter, that I account it any displeasure done me to be contradicted in print, but as it leads to the attainment of anything more true, shall esteem it a benefit; and shall know how to return his civility and fair argument in such a sort, as he shall confess that to do so is my choice, and to have done thus was my chance.

Poor Milton! if one is irritated by his humourless invective and sarcasm it is impossible not at times to be touched by the naïvety with which he returns upon himself as one who says: "Indeed, indeed, this is not the tone in which I wish to write could I but meet with reasonable opponents."

Not even *Areopagitica*, so interesting to later generations, contributed to Milton's contemporary influence:

"It appears incredible", writes Haller, "that Milton's great plea for freedom of the Press should have failed of any mention whatever in the thousands of pages printed at the time, and abounding in specific references to hundreds of other publications, but the present writer is constrained to report that after a protracted search he has failed to find a single one. Surely if the appearance of *Areopagitica* were ever to be noted it should have been by Prynne in that chapter of his *Fresh Discovery* written according to Thomason's dating about six months after the publication of *Areopagitica*, and devoted to the recent attacks upon the printing ordinance. But Prynne assails Henry Robinson, Lilburne, and the anonymous tracts of Overton, completely ignoring Milton." "At no time was Milton persecuted as others were for violation of the ordinance.... Milton was to be sure cited once in the Commons and once in the Lords but nothing came of the matter in either case."[1]

Mr Haller sees in the last-mentioned fact a proof that Milton was not regarded by the Presbyterians as one particularly dangerous. But there may be another reason. He may have had protectors. For if Milton is not found among the sectaries who were making themselves troublesome, and were frequently in trouble themselves, it was, I suggest, because they were moving in a different direction from that which Milton was to take. They were moving towards democracy, were the forerunners of later radicals. Milton was not. Even in the later *Defensio*, where he is vindicating the sovereignty of the people, he is quite explicit that the true people are not the mob but the great middle class. As he loosened himself from the Presbyterians Milton moved towards the Left certainly; but the opponents of Presbyterian intolerance were men of many kinds, not only fanatic

[1] *Op. cit.* p. 135.

Lilburnes and Levellers or forerunners of later democracy like Walwyn and Overton, but also men of higher
standing, social and financial, the forerunners of the later
Whig Oligarchy. Now Milton, it must be remembered, was a man of means and leisure with friends and
acquaintances among aristocratic families. Moreover,
the whole bent of his mind, and the direction given to
it by his studies, Biblical and Classical, made him an
aristocrat politically in the sense of the word as used by
Aristotle; in that sense only, for he is contemptuous
enough of the claims of hereditary aristocracy unsup-
ported by ability and character.

The interval between 1644, when his early pamphleteering closed, and 1649 was the crisis of Milton's
life. He was free to turn back to literary pursuits and
might have abandoned politics for ever. He permitted
the publication of his early poems (1645), he composed
some sonnets, and it *may* have been now that he drew
up the list of subjects for a possible drama or epic contained in the Trinity College manuscript.[1] It is usual to
place them earlier, between his return from Italy and the
first of the prelatical pamphlets, and I have accepted that
date, which is supported by the spellings in the manuscript. On the other hand there is some evidence
in the choice of subjects and the occasional indications
of how they are to be treated that suggests a mind full
of just those themes with which he has dealt in the prelatical and the marriage tracts. Observe some of the
comments, for they seem to me eloquent: "Edwin son
of Edgar for lust deprived of his kingdom, or rather by
faction of monks whom he hated; together [with] the

---

[1] That the poem, dramatic or epic, was in his mind is clear from the
statement in *Tetrachordon* : " I have yet a store of gratitude laid up, which
cannot be exhausted, and such thanks they may perhaps live to be, as shall
more than whisper to the next age."

imposter Dunstan." Again: "The slaughter of the
monks of Bangor by Edelfride stirred up, as is said, by
Ethelbert, and he by Austin the monk, because the
Britons would not receive the rites of the Roman
Church...which must begin with the convocation of
British clergie by Austen to determine superfluous
points which by them was refused." Again: "Edgar
slaying Ethelwold for false play in wooing wherein may
be set out his pride and lust which he thought to close
[? cloke] by favouring monks and building monasteries,
also the disposition of woman in Elfrida towards her
husband." Note these last words and add one that I
passed over in order to connect it with this: "Eduard son
of Edgar murdered by his stepmother. To which may be
inserted the tragedie stirred up betwixt the monks and
priests about marriage." These passages suggest that
they were set down when Milton's mind was still full of
two themes, still ready to grow passionate over them,
viz. prelates, including both priests and Presbyterians;
and marriage, women. What drew him back to politics
is not certain, but it is conjecturable. In 1646 his wife
sought and was granted a reconciliation, and with her
family she took refuge under his roof. To meet perhaps
the greater expense Milton increased the number of his
pupils, and among them were young men of family. It
was from the more aristocratic and influential wing of
the republicans that Milton must have been approached,
for with them he threw in his lot and became no longer
a free-lance but a recognised champion of the cause, and
the *sole* champion and vindicator of the final act in which
ended the long drawn out negotiations between Charles,

Presbyterian Parliament, and Independent, Sectarian Army—the death of the King and proclamation of the Republic. That it was by request Milton wrote *The Tenure of Kings and Magistrates* (Feb. 13, 1648–9, begun before but not printed till after the fatal day) is almost proved by its careful printing, with more than ordinary attention to Milton's peculiar spellings, by Matthew Symmons, the printer in chief, as he soon became, to the Commonwealth.[1] That it was not licensed would be part of the arrangement to make the works appear entirely a spontaneous production. For the *Eikonoklastes* (Oct. 6, 1649) was confessedly written to order and "Published by Authority". But whether ordered or not both were composed with Milton's full approval.

There is no use to-day discussing the constitutional questions and questions of political philosophy raised by Milton and by the fact of the execution. There never was any constitutional question to discuss. The execution was a revolutionary act, but so was the war. From the moment the first shot was fired the constitution was in suspense and would be recast by whichever side was victorious. Whoever lost would pay the penalty; "heads would roll", as Hitler used to say.

[1] And it at least brought him into the notice of the ruling men as none of his earlier works had done: "When I was released from these engagements, and thought that I was about to enjoy a period of uninterrupted ease, I turned my thoughts to a continued history of my country, from the earliest times to the present period. I had already finished four books when after the subversion of the monarchy, and the establishment of a republic, I was surprised by an invitation from the Council of State who desired my services in the office for foreign affairs. A book appeared soon after, which was ascribed to the King, and contained the most invidious charges against the parliament. I was ordered to answer it; and opposed the Iconoclast to his Icon." *Defensio Secunda,* trans. by Robert Fellowes.

The only question, and one impossible to answer, is whether it was better for England that Charles's head should roll or Cromwell's. Charles's was the more beautiful certainly. Cromwell's head did ultimately roll, but by that time, as Carlyle says, it had ceased entirely to interest himself, he was quite done with it; nor was his work to be so easily undone. However momentous for himself the step that Milton took in becoming, as Gardiner says, the sole literary champion of the new republic, it was a quite consistent development of his thought from the outset. For from the outset he had looked for more than the abolition of the Bishops, he had looked for a clean sweep in Church and State—a Church every member of which should be a priest in holy orders; a State which should regulate the life of the people in all important respects from education to pastimes, while refraining from any interference with the freedom of speech of the subjects. Milton would combine the licence of criticism of America with the strict regulation of Soviet Russia.

If he had hoped at first that, if not the people generally, yet at any rate a large recognised party would be with him, the storm raised by his tracts on marriage and the bitter opposition of the Presbyterian party to any toleration had disillusioned him; and, combined with his own temperament and the study of the Bible and of the Greek and Roman classics, had prepared him to accept an aristocratic republic, the rule, neither of hereditary kings nor of the mob, but of the wisest and best in the State—an ideal so pleasing to contemplate, so difficult to secure. Both the Bible and the Classics

pointed in the same direction, the former not by any
theory of government, for the Jews never had any but of
a theocracy; to develope any political philosophy based
on reason and experience was the work of the Greeks.
But in the Bible Milton found in abundance support for
the view that God raised up men for his own purposes,
as he inspired poets and prophets such as Milton believed he was or might be. The Presbyterians, he writes
in *The Tenure of Kings and Magistrates*, "protest against
those that talk of bringing him [the King] to justice,
which is the sword of God, superior to all mortal things,
*in whose hands soever by apparent signs his testified will is
to put it*". The Parliament and the Army "are in the
glorious way wherein Victory and Justice hath set them,
the only warrants throughout all ages, next under immediate revelation, to exercise supreme power, in those
proceedings which hitherto appeared equal to what hath
been done in any age or nation heretofore, justly or
magnanimously". This is the religious and ethical
ground on which he will justify the conduct of the
Regicides; the view to which he gave his final allegiance
even in the last days, in *Samson Agonistes*. God inspires
great men to do what cannot always be justified on
normal grounds of conduct or policy. "For if all human
power to execute, not accidentally but intendedly, the
wrath of God, upon evil doers without exception, be of
God, then that power, whether ordinary or, if that fail,
extraordinary so executing that intent of God is lawful
and not to be resisted." Such is Milton's doctrine, a
dangerous one that might be used to justify Lenin or
Mussolini or Hitler alike, the justification of success.

Yet it is hard to deny that in revolution as in war men must do many things they would not approve of in normal circumstances; and those of late who have been most condemnatory of war have been the first to condone the cruelties of revolution in Russia. Facts will never quite square with our moral principles or prejudices.

CHAPTER IV

The dismissal of Parliament—Milton and Cromwell

MILTON then deliberately returned to the political field, and that as the champion of a minority, but not to tie himself to any sect or leader. In politics as in religion he was to follow his own star. He might support Cromwell, but that support would not be unconditional. He might sympathise in their aims with the extremer sects, Independents, Baptists, even Quakers, but he enlisted with none of them. He *was* a sect: "I have never known that time in England when men of truest religion were not accounted sectaries." His faith was in the few, the heroic: "I confess there are but few, and those men of great wisdom and courage that are either desirous of liberty or capable of using it." But he would follow those few whom he deemed thus desirous and capable in the hope of their achieving the great work in Church and State of which he dreamed, but only so long as they seemed to him to be in the right way. Those he followed were, he believed, chosen of God to do a great work; he to witness and exhort; he also in the end to celebrate. But if they faltered he would denounce. Even Cromwell would be no "Führer" to be followed blindly.

Of the style in which Milton writes in these later pamphlets, and especially in the Latin *Defensiones*—and

above all in those parts in which he mauls poor Salmasius
and later Morus—I need not speak. One cannot call
these outbursts prophetic, an anger of the spirit. They
derive rather from the Humanists and the manner of
the Jesuits in their attacks on Scaliger.[1] To be able to
write in this manner was one of what Pattison calls, in
another connection, the rewards of a classical education.
These works interest us now only for the autobiographical interludes, the descriptions of the great men whom
Milton reckoned the deliverers of their country, his
Heroes, and by the knowledge they supply of Milton's
own ideals.

Of the great men whom he exalts—Bradshaw, Fairfax, Fleetwood, Lambert, Overton and others—one
name is pre-eminent, Oliver Cromwell. In estimating
Milton's consistency and conduct aright the crucial
factor is his attitude to Cromwell. Masson exaggerates
when he maintains that to Milton "Cromwell, to the

[1] "In 1605 Carolus Scribanius, Rector of the Jesuit College at Ant-
werp, produced the *Amphitheatrum Honoris.* The Amphitheatre is not
directed against Scaliger only; it includes the Calvinists generally. It is
difficult to give the English reader any idea of this production. It must
suffice to say that it is one of the most shamelessly beastly books which have
ever disgraced the printing press. The leading characters among the Re-
formed are brought up one after another, and the most filthy imputations
alleged against them, without the smallest evidence, or the pretence of it.
Even the titles of its chapters could not be reproduced in these pages. In
any moral condition of society the compiler of such a mass of ordure would
have been driven from among men as a pollution of his species. But
fifty years of Jesuit reaction had told terribly on the moral sense of
Europe. Scribanius was a defender of the Church, that was enough....
Good men were aghast, and recoiled from the Amphitheatre of *Horror*;
but the Catholic public applauded; and when an attempt was made to get
the sale of the book prohibited in France, Henri IV interfered in its
favour, and sent the author a message of encouragement, and letters of
naturalization as a citizen." Pattison, *Essays,* I, 190–1.

last, was our chief of men, the very greatest and noblest Englishman of that time". Cromwell was the greatest of those to whom Milton, turning away from the Presbyterians, looked for the work of deliverance; but he too (as we shall see) faltered and turned aside when he supported the granting of tithes to the clergy and when he dreamed of the kingship. For the second turning-point in Milton's life—the first being when he swore allegiance to the extremer republicans and wrote *The Tenure of Kings and Magistrates*—was the dismissal by Cromwell of the Parliament, or what remained of it, in 1653. Here again it was for Cromwell a matter of "you" or "me". The passing of the bill, the discussion of which Cromwell interrupted, would have been followed, says Gardiner, "by the threatened adjournment to November, and in the second place by the dismissal of Cromwell and the appointment of Fairfax as his successor. Fairfax in power would bring with him the domination of the hated Presbyterians with their notorious intolerance."

What was Milton's attitude towards this second act of Cromwell "as a destroyer" (Gardiner)? The way he spoke, after the death of Cromwell and the restoration of the Rump, implies that he had disapproved of Cromwell's action.

"I will begin with telling you", he writes in *A Letter to a Friend* (1659), "how I was overjoyed when I heard that the army, under the working of God's holy spirit, as I thought and still hope well, had been so far wrought to Christian humility and self-denial as to confess in public their back-sliding from the good old cause, and to shew the fruits of their repentance in the righteousness of their restoring the old famous parliament which they had without just authority dissolved; I call it the famous parliament though not the harmless since none well-affected but will confess they have deserved much more of these nations than they have undeserved."

These last words may be meant to suggest some defence of his approval at the time of what he now condemns, and calls in another pamphlet of the same year "a short but scandalous night of interruption". For Milton had in 1653 continued in Cromwell's service when others withdrew from public life; and it was in the second *Defensio* (1654) that he wrote his great panegyric on Cromwell and in the course of the eulogy defended his dismissal of Parliament:

> But when you saw that the business was artfully procrastinated, that every one was more intent on his own selfish interest than on the public good, that the people complained of the disappointments which they had experienced, and the fallacious promises by which they had been gulled, that they were the dupes of a few overbearing individuals, you put an end to their domination. . . . In this state of desolation you, O Cromwell! alone remained to conduct the government, and to save the country.

It is impossible to reconcile these statements. But certain things must be taken into consideration. Everything that Milton wrote in 1659–60 was written when he was fighting desperately for a cause to which he had devoted himself, body and soul. Secondly, Milton's feelings in 1653 were those of all that part of the nation which dreaded the return of Presbyterian intolerance. Cromwell's action, says Gardiner, was approved not only by those who, with Harrison at their head, were looking

for a Fifth Monarchy when the earth was to be ruled by
the saints and not by elected parliaments, but also by
the people who looked for and were promised by the
preachers lower taxation, peace with the Dutch, and
reform of the law in such a way as to offer justice to the
poor.[1] "Cromwell himself for the last time in his life

---

[1] See also what Milton says of the Parliament in the digression at
the opening of the third book of the *History of Britain*. The paragraphs
were omitted in all editions before the two-volume folio of 1738:

"Of these who sway'd most in the late troubles, few words as to
this point may suffice. They had armies, leaders and successes to thir
wish; but to make use of so great advantage was not thir skill. To
other causes therefore and not to want of force, or warlike manhood
in the Brittains...we must impute the ill husbanding of those fair
opportunities which might seem to have put liberties, so long desir'd
like a bird into thir hands.... For a parliament being call'd, and as was
thought many things to redress, the people with great courage and ex-
pectation to be now eas'd of what discontented them chose to thir behoof
in parliament such as they thought best affected to the public good, and
some indeed men of wisdome and integrity; the rest, and to be sure
the greatest part, whom wealth and ample possessions or bold and active
ambition rather than merit had commended to the same place, when
once the superficial zeale and popular fumes that acted thir new majesty
were cool'd and spent in them, straite every one betook himself, setting
the commonwealth behind and his private ends before, to doe as his
owne profit or ambition led him. Then was justice delay'd and soone
after deny'd, spite and favour determin'd all: hence faction, then
treacherie both at home and in the field, ev'ry where wrong & oppression, foule and dishonest things committed daylie, or maintain'd in
secret or in op'n. Some who had bin call'd from shops and warehouses
without other merit to sit in supreme councels and committees as thir
breeding was fell to hucster the common-wealth; others did there after
as men could sooth and humour them best: so that hee only who could
give most, or under cover of hypocritical zeal insinuate basest enjoy'd
unworthylie the rewards of learning and fidelity, or escap'd the punish-
ment of his crimes and misdeeds. The votes and ordinances which
men look'd should have contain'd the repealing of bad laws & the
immediate constitution of better, resounded with nothing else but new
impositions, taxes, excises, yearly, monthly, weekly, not to reckon the
offices, gifts and preferments bestow'd and shar'd among themselves."
So Milton continues in his indictment of the rule of the Parliament,

became the most applauded man in England and that attested not only by the newspapers but by the foreign ambassadors." Thirdly, Milton's approval of Cromwell at the time was qualified by certain conditions which he states frankly. In the second *Defensio* he approves, as I have said, the dismissal of the Parliament and is also distrustful of the call for a freely elected parliament:

For it is of little consequence, O citizens, by what principles you are governed, either in acquiring liberty or in retaining it when acquired. And unless that liberty, which is of such a kind

the Long Parliament, "the old famous parliament" of the *Letter to a Friend* (1659). From Parliament he passes to the Church and the Westminster Assembly, and from that to the radical faults of the British people: "For Britain (to speak a truth not oft spoken) as it is a land fruitful enough of men stout and courageous in warr, so is it naturallie not over fertil of men able to govern justlie & prudently in peace; trusting onlie on thir Mother-witt, as most doo, & consider not that civilitie, prudence, love of the public more then of money or vaine honour are to this soil out-landish; grow not here but in minds well implanted with solid and elaborate breeding; too impolitic els and too crude, if not headstrong and intractable to the industrie and vertue of executing or understanding true civil government. Valiant indeed and prosperous to win a field but to know the end and reason of winning, injudicious and unwise, in good and bad success alike unteachable. For the sunn, which we want, ripens witts as well as fruits; and as wine and oyle are imported to us from abroad, so must ripe understanding and many civil vertues bee imported into our minds from forren writings & examples of best ages: we shall else miscarry still and come short in the attempt of any great enterprise." So far has Milton wandered from his first glorification of God's Englishmen in the *Areopagitica*. So far is he from identifying a free constitution with a democratic government. Milton, like Carlyle, looks for Heroes if (like Carlyle) he is loth to find a complete hero in anyone who differs from John Milton. Mr Belloc accuses Milton of insularity, of accepting the severance of England from the Continent. But surely, alike in literature and politics and religion, his view is or would be European, though Protestant. In literature it is European without limitation of religion. Even our English Sabbatarianism he finds an unnecessary separation of our Protestant Churches from those of the Continent.

as arms can neither procure nor take away, which alone is the fruit of piety, of justice, of temperance, and unadulterated virtue, shall have taken deep root in your hearts and minds, there will not long be wanting one who will snatch from you by treachery what you have acquired by arms. War has made many great whom peace makes small.

His trust and hope is in the great men. In modern terms what Milton wanted was the dictatorship of the proletariat, that is for the proletariat or at least for the middle classes. "Nothing is more agreeable to the order of nature, or more for the interest of mankind, than that the less should yield to the greater, not in numbers, but in wisdom and in virtue." Among these he reckons Cromwell and himself:

He alone is worthy of the appellation who either does great things, or teaches how they may be done, or describes them with a suitable majesty when they have been done; but those only are great things which tend to render life more happy, which increase the innocent enjoyments and comforts of existence, or which pave the way to a state of future bliss more permanent and more pure.

Cromwell belongs to the first class; Milton and others to the second; Milton alone to the third, as he still hopes. For I am disposed to think, though it cannot be proved, that if Milton postponed till as late as 1658 beginning work on *Paradise Lost*, it was because he still dreamed of a great poem dealing directly or symbolically with the liberation of England, the reform of reformation. As Mr Tillyard says, the second *Defensio* is written in the same spirit and temper as the first books of *Paradise Lost*; and I would go further (and I think that Mr Tillyard leans to the same view) and say that in this *Defensio* (or both the Defences taken together) Milton felt that he had in a way fulfilled his first intention of a poem on the exploits of the English people and statesmen; and so bade farewell to the subject:

I have delivered my testimony, I would almost say have erected a monument that will not readily be destroyed, to the reality of those singular and mighty achievements which were above all praise. As the epic poet who adheres at all to the rules of that species of composition does not profess to describe the whole life of the hero whom he celebrates but only some particular action of his life, as the resentment of Achilles, at Troy, the return of Ulysses, or the coming of Aeneas into Italy; so it will be sufficient, either for my justification or apology, that I have heroically celebrated at least one exploit of my countrymen; I pass by the rest for who could recite the achievements of a whole people?

Words could hardly imply more clearly that Milton chose to think that, in a way he had not foreseen, this first great project had been completed. He had written his epic on an historical theme, not Arthur, nor any other King or Knight before the Conquest chosen as the pattern of a Christian hero. No; but his theme had been no less a one than the bringing of a king to justice, not by way of assassination, nor in the wild explosion of the bestial passions of a mob, but with all deliberation and dignity by men fitted for that high calling of God and doing a deed exemplary to the nations. And these men, not Cromwell alone, but Cromwell surrounded by faithful generals and counsellors, were Milton's "pattern of a Christian hero". If this be so, then we must see in *Paradise Lost* something other than the fulfilment of his original intention, something to

which he passed when that had been achieved in ways
decreed by God and Destiny. To that I shall return
again.

But even in this work, in the utterance of the moment
of his fullest sympathy with the regicides, Milton's
eulogy of Cromwell is not without qualification and
warning. It is a noble eulogy. If it has been suggested
that Milton took from Cromwell some of the traits in
his Satan, I confess it seems to me that there is a closer
kinship between the Cromwell he here celebrates and
the Christ of his own *Paradise Regained*, the picture of a
man who has conquered the meaner passions and gained
a complete mastery over himself:

"He was a soldier disciplined to perfection in the knowledge of
himself. He had either extinguished or by habit learned to subdue, the whole host of vain hopes, fears, and passions which infest
the soul. He first acquired the government of himself, over himself gained the most signal victories, so that in the first day he took
the field against the external enemy he was a veteran in arms
consummately practised in the toils and exigencies of wars." "The
whole surface of the British Empire has been the scene of his
exploits and the theatre of his triumphs."

The appeal which follows is even nobler in tone, and
into it Milton has instilled, with a freedom which does
honour to Cromwell and to himself, a warning, a clear
indication that there were limits to Milton's acceptance
of the rule of the hero of the great *coup d'état*. He must
not make himself a tyrant, "for such is the nature of
things, that he who entrenches on the liberty of others
is the first to lose his own and become a slave". He
must associate himself with the "companions of your

dangers and your toils", whereupon follows the eulogy
of Fleetwood, Lambert, Hawley, Desborough, Overton:
"To these men, whose talents are so splendid, and whose
worth has been so thoroughly tried, you would without
doubt do right to trust the protection of our liberties;
nor would it be easy to say to whom they might more
easily be entrusted." Moreover, Cromwell must carry
out Milton's programme, realise his ideals of a complete
separation of Church and State, the reduction and sim-
plification of the laws,[1] "a better provision for the
education of youth", and the permission of "the free
discussion of truth without any hazard to the author or
any subjection to the caprice of the individual".[2] From
the eulogy of, and appeal to, Cromwell Milton passes
to the English people themselves, beseeching or warning them that, having passed through the fire, they
should not now perish in the smoke:

"For instead of fretting with vexation, or thinking that you
can lay the blame on any one but yourselves, know to be free is
the same thing as to be pious, to be wise, to be temperate and just,
to be frugal and abstinent, and lastly to be magnanimous and

[1] The tone of Milton's appeal to Cromwell, and the warnings with
which he invested his eulogy, were clearly recognised at the time, for
example by Morus in his reply: "All which has so elated you that you
would be reckoned next after the first man in England and sometimes
put yourself higher than the supreme Cromwell himself, whom you name
familiarly without giving him any title of rank, whom you lecture under
the guise of praising him, to whom you dictate laws, assign boundaries to
his rights, suggest counsels, and even hold out threats if he shall not be-
have accordingly. You grant him arms and rule; you claim genius and
the gown for yourself. He is to be called great, you say, who either does
great things, Cromwell, to wit; or teaches great things, Milton on Divorce,
to wit; or writes worthily of them, the same twice great Milton, I suppose,
in his *Defence of the English People*."

[2] Masson, v, 160.

brave; so to be the opposite of all these is the same as to be a slave." "If you think slavery an intolerable evil learn obedience to reason and the government of yourselves."

Then follows what I have cited as his claim to have written his historical poem on the great theme of the vindication of liberty by England.[1]

[1] The *Defensio Secunda* was published in May 1654 and therefore was presumably the work of the early months of the year. Now the Barebones Parliament was already in serious difficulties by the month of November 1653, over ecclesiastical matters, especially the abolition of tithes, but also over proposals to abolish the Court of Chancery and generally to hasten and cheapen the business of the law. In that month the officers of the army had already prepared "a draft instrument offering Cromwell the government with the title of King; but on December 1st Cromwell, still averse from a second military expulsion, refused the offer". When the Parliament was persuaded, by somewhat of a trick, to vote its own extinction, the Instrument was revived but with now the title of Protector for Cromwell (Dec. 15, 1653). Now what was Milton's feeling about the dismissal of the Barebones Parliament? He mentions it very shortly after the Long Parliament: "A new Parliament is called, the privilege of voting is allowed to those only to whom it was proper to allow it; the elected meet; and having harassed one another for a while with their dissentions and altercations, and most of them being of opinion that they were unfit persons, and not equal to undertakings of such magnitude, they dissolve themselves. Cromwell, we are deserted: you alone remain." But if I follow the historians this is not a quite ingenuous account of what happened, nor perhaps of what Milton himself felt. It was not because they did nothing that the Parliament fell into disrepute, but because it did or threatened to do too much in things ecclesiastical and legal; and its self-dismissal was brought about by a trick. "Before they had been a month in session they passed a resolution that the Court of Chancery should be wholly taken away and abolished; and after three bills had been brought in and dropped for carrying this resolution into act, they read a second for summarily deciding cases then pending, and arranging that for the future the ordinary suits in chancery should be promptly dispatched at a cost of from twenty to forty shillings.... The power of patrons to present to livings was taken away...they indicated their intention to abolish tithe and the endowment of ministers of religion by the State. This led to the crisis.... The army, the lawyers, the clergy, the holders of property, all felt themselves attacked; and the Lord-General himself perceived, in his own words, afterwards, that the issue

Milton thus made himself in the *Defensio Secunda* the mouthpiece of the extreme Puritanism which, Gardiner indicates, reached its high-water mark in Cromwell's nominated parliament:

of this assembly would have been the subversion of the laws, and of all the liberties of the nation, the destruction of the ministers of the gospel, in short the confusion of all things." So the Lord-General may have come to feel, though in the famous colloquy with Ludlow when he held forth for an hour on the 110th Psalm he had indicated that his great desire was "a thorough reformation of the clergy and the law...the law as it is now constituted serves only to maintain the lawyer, and to encourage the rich to oppress the poor" (Morley, *Cromwell*, 1900). What is quite certain is that, whatever Cromwell may have come to think, these were just the things which Milton, like Carlyle whose account of the Barebones Parliament forms an amusing contrast to Morley's, desired and desired passionately. In sentiment he is a Barebones Parliament man, and if Cromwell governs now alone it is, Milton hopes, to carry out these things by his own strong hand; that he will not assume the title of King but be content with that of Protector ("Your achievements surpass every degree even of admiration, and much more do they surpass every title: they rise above the popular atmosphere of titles as the tops of pyramids hide themselves in the clouds"), that he will "take away all power from the Church —and power will never be wanting as long as there shall be money, the poison of the Church, the quinsy of truth, as long as there shall be hire for preaching the gospel, coercively collected even from those who have no disposition to pay it"; that Cromwell should introduce fewer new laws than he abrogates old ones. And so on through the whole gamut of the extremists' demands, except that Milton makes no concession to democratic demands for new elections or the rule of the majority. For the majority he has nothing but contempt: "Who denies that there may be times in which the vicious may constitute the majority of the citizens, who would rather follow Catiline or Antony than the more virtuous part of the Senate? But are not good citizens on this account to oppose the bad with vigour and decision? Ought they not to be less deterred by the smallness of their numbers than they are animated by the goodness of their cause?" Milton was no constitutional or philosophical pedant. He was eager for certain results, a purified Church (as he understood it) and a well-ordered State, and to obtain these he was willing, like Carlyle, to go a long way in the direction of an authoritarian State, if the State would only do what he wishes, and let every man have his say. But his acceptance of Cromwell's *coup-d'état* was clearly provisional. The second defence was a purely personal document, no commission of the government's like the

A puritanism which on the one hand rejected all mundane influences and rights over the individual conscience and upheld in opposition to the state a purely voluntary ecclesiastical system; and which on the other hand strove to use the absolute powers, which it had under the most unlikely circumstances acquired, to force this system—or rather this absence of system—on a nation which had never demanded it and was never likely to demand it within any reasonable limits of time.

And Cromwell did not fulfil Milton's hopes. He regarded Milton's expostulations just as much or as little as a Prime Minister to-day may or may not heed a letter to *The Times*. During the next five years Milton was an official writing occasional letters, the most notable being those that dealt with the massacre of the Waldenses. His duties were decreasing and with them his salary. He continued the unedifying quarrel with More in his *Pro se Defensio* (1655), but in no pamphlet did he either champion Cromwell's government or criticise it, even when Cromwell committed what in his eyes was the great betrayal of restoring the tithes to the clergy. But his hopes were not easily quenched. On Cromwell's death he turns back to Parliament, first Richard's elected Parliament to which he addressed his *Treatise of*

first. It had two ends in view, a personal vindication and a warning, a programme; for the new ruler. Milton's position during the next four years must have been a somewhat ambiguous one, but whose is not in a revolution? Mr Tillyard claims for the *Defensio Secunda* that it is the greatest of Milton's prose works and one of the greatest of the world's rhetorical writings; and he finds in it a fuller and more certain note than ever before. The first half of this judgement would need some qualifications from consideration of the depths to which Milton's humour and invective descend. The second I should qualify so far as to say that I detect in the last and greatest part of the speech (as one may call it) an unmistakable note of uneasiness, a growing feeling of uncertainty regarding both the rulers and the English people.

Civil Power in Ecclesiastical Causes (February 1659),
then to the Rump, which he welcomes "after a short
but scandalous night of interruption". To the end he
fought a desperate battle, with less and less belief in the
people; and to Monk at last recommends what is
practically the Soviet system of Russia to-day—a permanent Central Council and permanent County Councils. Any element of free election, after the manner
suggested by Harrington, he regards with extreme ill
will. But the mass of Englishmen were sick of these
controversies and of being driven in the name of liberty.
The good old cause went down to the ringing of bells
and roasting of rumps. Milton went into hiding. His
Defensio and the *Ikonoklastes* were burned, but he escaped
with his life.

"At his Majesty's happy return", writes Marvell, in his controversy with the renegade Parker, "J. M. did partake, even as you
yourself did, for all your huffing, of his royal clemency, and has
ever since expiated himself in a retired silence. Whether it were
my foresight or my good fortune I never contracted any friendship or confidence with you; but then it was you frequented
J. M. incessantly, and haunted his house day by day. What discourses you there used he is too generous to remember."

To *Paradise Lost* then Milton came finally in a very
different spirit from that in which he had dreamed of an
historical epic, symbolising the great achievements of
the English people, a "song to generations", a poem in
which great deeds were to be celebrated "with a suitable
majesty". *Paradise Lost* was to be something very
different. An historical subject was out of the question
for Milton as he sat in silence expiating his offences.

Even parts of the *History of England* which referred too obviously to the course of events during the Rebellion, the lamentable failure of the English Parliament and people, had to be cut out when the *History* was printed. No; Milton would take up the Biblical story, what the Dutch poet calls "the tragedy of tragedies", and make of it what one must call an arraignment of mankind from Adam to the Day of Judgement—Man's fatal weakness, his proneness to subordinate reason to passion, what Mr Tillyard calls man's triviality, and a novelist to-day has said: "If triviality takes an important place in the world, if it is the chief barrier between men and God then triviality is important....No corruption is more easily spread than that of trivial-mindedness." Calvin's doctrine of predestination, of election, takes in Milton's mind an aspect which reflects more the spirit of the Renaissance than of Christianity, though it is not Macchiavellian but ethical, such a view as Carlyle would endeavour to adumbrate in his doctrine of the hero who must be also a good man. Only the few, that is Milton's conviction, are capable of preserving the Liberty which Adam was endowed with but lost; which Christ the perfect Man preserved unshaken; which Samson reasserted at the cost of his life and the life of his enemies.

Liberty hath a sharp and double edge, fit only to be handled by just and virtuous men; to bad and dissolute it becomes a mischief unwieldy in their hands; neither is it given but by them who have the happy skill to know what is grievous and unjust to a people and how to remove it wisely; what good laws are wanting, and how to frame them substantially, that good men may enjoy the freedom which they merit and the bad the curb which they need.

Milton was quite prepared for a dictatorship of the proletariat by the virtuous. "If the greater part value not freedom but will degenerately forego, is it just or reasonable that most voices against the main end of government should enslave the less number that would be free?" That is Milton's conviction. The good are few; the heroes fitted to rule men still fewer; fewer still the poets fitted to sing of great deeds. It is his own bitter experience, his arraignment of the English people who had passed through the fire to perish in the smoke, which he carries into his reading of human history. Some critics have found a reflection of Milton in his Satan. He is much more closely to be identified with his own picture of the Deity, just but stern; not inexorable (as Milton had shown in his treatment of Mary Powell and her family):

> To prayer, repentance and obedience due,
> Though but endeavoured with sincere intent,
> Mine ear shall not be slow, mine eye not shut;

scornful of any conduct or excuse for conduct that savoured of weakness. Milton's mind has passed through the cycle which Dr Charles describes in the progress of Jewish prophetic and apocalyptic literature, postponing to a remoter and remoter future, and ultimately to the coming of a new heaven and a new earth, the hopes for a Messianic Kingdom. Milton too had hoped for a new era, a second coming: "Come forth out of thy royal chambers, O Prince of all the Kings of the Earth, put on the visible robes of thy imperial Majesty, take up that unlimited scepter which the

Almighty Father hath bequeathed thee; for now the voice of the Bride calls thee and all creatures sigh to be renewed." But that dream had dislimned and disappeared leaving no rack behind. Only in another world than this shall the hopes of good men find fulfilment:

> So shall the world go on
> To good malignant, to bad men benign,
> Under her own weight groaning, till the Day
> Appear of respiration to the just,
> And vengeance to the wicked, at return
> Of Him so lately promis'd to thy aid,
> The woman's seed, obscurely then foretold,
> Now amplier known thy Saviour and thy Lord,
> Last in the clouds from Heaven to be reveal'd
> In glory of the Father, to dissolve
> Satan with his perverted world, then raise
> From the conflagrant mass, purg'd and refin'd
> New Heavens, new Earth, Ages of endless date
> Founded in righteousness and peace and love,
> To bring forth fruits, Joy and Eternal Bliss.

Only after the Day of Judgement, only in Heaven, will Milton's dream be fulfilled; and into Milton's Heaven only heroes are to enter. The mass of men are "Satan's perverted world". Milton's "song to generations" has become an arraignment of Man from Adam onwards. Milton and the great Puritans of the Commonwealth had little patience with the Herd:

> to be weak is miserable
> Doing or suffering;

"wicked therefore weak" Milton says of Satan, but he is too ready to convert the proposition universally and say "weak therefore wicked"; and of all ways of being weak none is more fatal than that of Adam:

> here only weak
> Against the charm of Beauty's powerful glance.

What I have yet to do therefore is to consider *Paradise Lost* and the two poems which followed as poetry and as prophetic poetry, for even as poetry there have been of late rather sweeping attempts at revaluation.

CHAPTER V

*The final return to poetry—Milton's early poems—
Paradise Lost—Its doctrine and its temper—The prophetic and the poetic in the poem—Milton's diction
and verse*

COMING thus to consider *Paradise Lost* and its
successors as poetry I reach the main theme of my
study—how far is Milton to be reckoned a prophetic
poet in the sense which I gave to that word in my
opening chapter, a poet putting into the language and
pattern of poetry his deepest intuitions as these have
been evoked by a great political and religious experience? To consider this question fully I must turn back
to those earlier poems which for my special purpose I
have hitherto passed over in silence, poems for which
the poet himself made no claim to any prophetic
burden, though the *Masque*, or *Comus* as it is generally
called, had an express didactic intention. It was, that
is to say, a poem meant not only to delight a courtly
audience on an official occasion, but to read a lesson to
the young and noble children about to enter that dark
wood haunted of Comus and his crew which is the
Court:

He will teach you, that good and bad have not
    One latitude in cloisters and in Court;
Indifferent there the greatest space hath got;
    Some pity is not good there, some vain disport,
On this side sin, with that place may comport.[1]

[1] John Donne, *To the Countess of Bedford.*

But the Puritan was not disposed to allow so wide a margin to things indifferent as the Catholic. About the Court Milton felt more as Spenser had done, or more severely:

> But they of love and of his sacred lere,
> (As it should be) all otherwise devise
> Then we poor shepherds are accustomed here,
> And him do sue and serve all otherwise.
> For with lewd speeches and licentious deeds
> His mighty mysteries do they prophane,
> And use his idle name to other needs
> But as a compliment for courting vaine.
> So him they do not serve as they professe,
> But make him serve to them for sordid uses.

I cannot bring myself to think with Mr Holly Hand-ford that the glorification of Virginity in *Comus* repre-sents in Milton a turning of his own thoughts and intentions away even from Marriage. It is to the young people for whom he is writing that he holds up the ideal to which he himself had been faithful in his youth. "Nor did I slumber over that place expressing such high rewards of ever accompanying the Lamb, with those celestial songs to others inapprehensible, but not to those who were not defil'd with women, which doubtless means fornication; for marriage must not be call'd a defilement." So he later recalls his own youthful and soaring thoughts on the problem of sex. But the lofty speech in which the Lady pronounces an apologia for Virginity was not thought by Lawes appropriate for the mouth of a young girl of thirteen, and it was omitted in performance. Didactic *Comus* is, but not prophetic—

that is its limitation as a great poem on the theme of temptation and chastity.

To return to the poetry as such, Milton was from his earliest days given the best and most careful education which his father could afford, at the hands of private tutors and at St Paul's School under the older and younger Gill, and finally at Cambridge. For the rhetorical and dialectical education of the Universities in his day Milton expressed, early and late, a profound contempt.

"How many despicable quibbles there are in grammar and rhetoric! One may hear the teachers of them talking sometimes like savages and sometimes like babies. What about logic? That is indeed the Queen of the Arts, if taught as it should be, but unfortunately how much foolishness there is in reason! Its teachers are not like men at all, but like finches which live on thorns and thistles!" "What am I to say of that branch of learning which the Peripatetics call metaphysics? It is not, as the authority of great men would have me believe, an exceedingly rich art; it is, I say, not an art at all, but a sinister rock, a quagmire of fallacies, devised to cause shipwreck and pestilence. These are the wounds... which the ignorance of gownsmen inflicts; and the monkish disease has already infected natural philosophy to a considerable extent; the mathematicians too are afflicted with a longing for the petty triumphs of demonstrative rhetoric."[1]

So, while still a student, Milton attacks the favourite studies and the dialectic method (the method whereby the student was called on to defend opposite propositions on the same general theme) of his Alma Mater. It is little wonder that he was not elected to a fellowship;

[1] *Milton's Correspondence and Academic Exercises*, Cambridge, 1932.

and to the end of his career the reform of education was one of the demands Milton pressed on Parliament and on Cromwell. Nevertheless, Milton submitted to the curriculum, and the sentences I have quoted are from Mrs Tillyard's translation of one of the academic, dialectic exercises which Milton wrote at Cambridge, and thought so well of himself as to print, with other of his writings, towards the end of his life. They are discussions, half serious, half humorous, on such themes as whether Day or Night is the more excellent, the Harmony of the Spheres, the Scholastic Philosophy; or such metaphysical themes as whether when a substance is destroyed there is any resolution into First Matter; or a rhetorical defence of learning. The last is an eloquent eulogy on two favourite Renaissance themes, the worth of learning, and the desire of fame, "that last infirmity of noble mind". But in general they are clever exercises in the subtleties of scholastic logic and rhetoric which established conclusions, but discovered and proved nothing.

But what I wish to indicate is that Milton's early poems, Latin and English, are poetic exercises of much the same kind, the English poems even more so perhaps than the Latin, for into the latter he does put a good deal of his experience and thought. If we recur to the rough division of poetry I made in my first chapter, poetry which may fairly be described in Pope's words as "What oft was thought but ne'er so well express'd"; poetry into which, in one way or another, argument, "discourse of reason" enters; and intuitional poetry,

poetry, whether personal in reference or on a public
theme, in which we feel that the poet is not arguing nor
yet merely given beautiful expression to accepted sentiments, but is speaking the language of the heart as we
say, the thoughts that rise from the interaction of reason,
and passion, and imagination, then these early poems
come under the first head. They are essentially works
of art, poems that delight us, not by any freshness of
thought subtle or profound, by any unusual depth of
feeling and intuition such as arrests us (to leave out
for the moment such *great* prophetic poetry as that of
the Hebrew poets or Aeschylus) in the best of Shakespeare's sonnets, in Wordsworth's lyrics and reflective
poems, in some of Shelley's most piercing lyrics. Of the
wonderful richness and perfection of the art there can
be no question. As I have said elsewhere, Keats's fine
odes are almost the only poems that give the same sense
of sensuous and imaginative richness and of perfection
of form, that is of evolution and changing but always
appropriate cadences.

What but a youthful experiment in poetic rhetoric is
the poem on the death of a child dying of a cough; and
to pass to the first perfect English poem that Milton
wrote, a poem delightful in delicacy of feeling and
beauty of movement, the Hymn *On the Morning of
Christ's Nativity*, is it very different? Milton explores
no fresh line of thought concerning God Made Man;
opens up no vein of personal feeling. What he does is
to play a number of exquisite variations on the familiar,
accepted themes: the coming of the child in winter; at

a moment when peace prevails throughout the world, when the gates of Janus are closed:

> No war or battle's sound
> Was heard the world around,
>   The idle spear and shield were high up hung;
> The hookèd chariot stood
> Unstain'd with hostile blood,
>   The trumpet spake not to the armèd throng.
> And Kings sat still with awful eye,
> As if they surely knew their sovereign Lord was by.

Then come the shepherds whom Milton thinks of as they are presented in pastoral poetry; the song of the angels and that old rhetorical theme, the music of the spheres; then the end of the oracles; the Virgin and the Babe—a series of delightful conceits on a familiar theme. Compare this with Donne's lines on

Good Friday, 1613. *Riding Westward.*

> Let man's soul be a sphere, and then in this
> The intelligence that moves devotion is,
> And as the other spheres, by being grown
> Subject to foreign motions, lose their own,
> And being by others hurried every day,
> Scarce in a day their natural form obey:
> Pleasure or business, so, our souls admit
> For their first mover, and are whirl'd by it.
> Hence is't that I am carried towards the West
> This day, when my soul's form bends toward the East.
> There I should see a sunne, by rising set,
> And by that setting endless day beget;
> But that Christ by this Crosse, did rise and fall,
> Sin had eternally benighted all.
> Yet dare I almost be glad, I do not see
> That spectacle of too much weight for mee.
> Who sees Gods face, that is self life, must die;

What a death were it then to see God die!
It made his own Lieutenant Nature shrinke,
It made his footstool crack, and the Sunne winke.
Could I behold those hands which span the Poles.
And turne all spheares at once, pierc'd with those holes?
Could I behold that endless height which is
Zenith to us and our Antipodes,
Humbl'd below us? or that blood which is
The seat of all our souls, if not of his,
Made durt of dust, or that flesh which was worn
By God for this apparel, rag'd and torn?
If on these things I durst not look, durst I
Upon his miserable mother cast mine eye,
Who was God's partner here, and furnish'd thus
Half of that Sacrifice, which ransom'd us?
Though these things, as I ride, be from mine eye,
They'are present yet unto my memory,
For that looks towards them; and thou lookst towards mee,
O Saviour as thou hang'st upon the tree;
I turn my back to thee, but to receive
Corrections, till thy mercy bid thee leave.
O think mee worth thine anger, punish mee,
Burne off my rusts, and my deformity,
Restore thine Image, so much, by thy grace,
That thou may'st know mee, and I'll turne my face.

Here are no charming variations on thoughts about
the Passion common to every Christian. Donne's mind
is set to work on the thought that he is turning his back
towards the earthly site of the Crucifixion, and on that
thought he proceeds to elaborate a series of surprises—
what is *there* happening and its significance for us, the
intolerableness of such a spectacle, its presence in his
memory, the turning of his back "to receive correction"
till he be fit to turn and *see*. That is "metaphysical"

poetry, not alone in virtue of the scholastic theory of the spheres, but of the whole evolution of the poem, not certainly "What oft was thought but ne'er so well express'd", nor yet, I venture to think, intuitional poetry (of which prophetic is a branch) in which the thoughts stream up from the depths of thought and feeling with no such suggestion of conscious elaboration by the help of wit and learning. This, and Donne's poems generally, illustrate what De Quincey chose to regard as specifically "rhetoric": "the art of aggrandising and bringing out into strong relief, by means of various and striking thoughts, some aspect of truth which of itself is supported by no spontaneous feelings, and therefore rests upon artificial aids", e.g. Scholastic philosophy.[1] Set it beside Emily Brontë's poem already cited "No coward soul is mine", and see clearly the distinction between passionate intuition and passionate dialectic and rhetoric. But one must not make one's distinctions too mutually exclusive. I am not prepared to deny Donne spontaneity, if that includes sincerity of feeling, although his elaboration of the feeling is subtle and full of surprises dialectical and rhetorical. Donne is one of those poets who are "naturally artificial; for them simplicity would be affectation". He is spontaneously subtle.

[1] "The first very eminent rhetorician in the English literature is Donne.... In saying *that*, however, we must remind our readers that we revert to the original use of the word *Rhetoric*, as laying the principal stress upon the management of the thoughts, and only a secondary one upon the ornaments of style. Few writers have shown a more extraordinary compass of powers than Donne; for he combined—what no other man has ever done—the last sublimation of dialectical subtlety and address with impassioned majesty." De Quincey, *Rhetoric*: Collected Works, ed. Masson, 1890, x. 101.

But to return to Milton, what is true of the Hymn is equally so of the other poems. *L'Allegro* and *Il Penseroso* are, Mr Tillyard has recently pointed out, poems suggested by one of Milton's own rhetorical Academic Prolusions, a dialectical discussion of the relative excellence of Day and Night. They are poetical variations on two moods of mind—delightful expressions of two sides of Milton's own temperament, exquisite in their selection, description or suggestion of appropriate details—appropriate, that is, to the mood studied—original in their difference of plan, of development, *L'Allegro* opening the progress of a day's experiences with the song of the lark, *Il Penseroso* at the hour when Philomel may

> deign a song,
> In her sweetest saddest plight,
> Smoothing the rugged brow of night.

But Milton attempts no philosophical estimate of the significance of the two diverse moods. Compare again, though the resemblances may be more remote, with Donne's perverse, and exaggerated if you like, but haunting *On St Lucie's Day*.

The most passionate and perfect of all these early poems is *Lycidas*, and what is *Lycidas* but a splendid experiment in a traditional form, the pastoral elegy as that had been composed by Theocritus, Bion, Moschus, Virgil, Clement Marot, Spenser, Drummond? This is the ground of Johnson's harsh verdict: "The form is that of a pastoral—easy, vulgar and therefore disgusting." Milton has indeed breathed into the poem a fresh note of passion, but just in those parts where the fate of

King leads him to reflection upon his own past intentions of entering the ministry and his hopes of writing a great poem. What Johnson overlooked was Milton's art, the fact that, whatever we may think of his choice of topics, "*Lycidas* is probably the most perfect piece of pure literature in existence because every word and phrase and line is sonorous, ringing and echoing with music" (Machen, *The Hill of Dreams*).

Lycidas was written in 1637. Between then and 1658 Milton, so far as we can trace, wrote nothing in English but a few occasional sonnets and some negligible translations from the Psalms. Mr Belloc has recently passed a very severe judgement on Milton's sonnets, as Dr Johnson did in his *Life of Milton* and in his remark to a lady that Milton could carve a Colossus but could not cut heads upon cherrystones. Mr Belloc's objection is a technical one, that Milton neglects what he calls, rather pontifically, the law of the sonnet, viz. that the fourteen lines should fall into two parts, corresponding to the octave and sextet, containing a statement and counterstatement. He affirms that Shakespeare has always followed this construction. A good example is Shakespeare's twenty-ninth sonnet:

> When in disgrace with fortune and men's eyes
> I all alone beweep my outcast state,

where, after enumerating his deficiencies compared with the qualities of other men, in the sestet he recovers his self-confidence with the thought:

> Yet in these thoughts myself almost despising
> Haply I think on thee, and then my state

(Like to the lark at break of day arising)
From sullen earth sings hymns at Heaven's gate,
For thy sweet love remember'd such wealth brings,
That then I scorn to change my state with kings.

Another example is Milton's sonnet:

How soon hath time, the subtle thief of youth,
Stol'n on his wing my three and twentieth year

where, with the sestet, comes the turn

Yet be it less or more, or soon or slow,
It shall be still in strictest measure even, etc.

But quite as often as not the turn in a sonnet of Shake-speare's does not come till the final couplet, as in the thirtieth:

When to the sessions of sweet silent thought

ending:

But if the while I think on thee (dear friend)
All losses are restored, and sorrows end.

A somewhat epigrammatic close, which one gets again in Milton's sonnet on the death of his second wife:

But, O! as to embrace me she enclin'd,
I wak'd, she fled, and day brought back my night.

And even in this he avoids the final rhyme. To the pointed roof effect (with one side rather longer than the other) which Mr Belloc commends Milton prefers the arch or curve, a short poem in which one feels from the first line that he is working out a single thought. This effect he does secure and in doing so begins the use of that device which he was to employ in his maturer blank verse, namely the carrying over of the sense from line to line with the use of strong medial pauses. In the Cromwell sonnet the turn which Mr Belloc demands comes in the middle of a line:

> Yet much remains
> To conquer still: Peace hath her victories
> No less renown'd than war; new foes arise
> Threatening to bind our souls with secular chains.
> Help us to save free conscience from the paw
> Of hireling wolves, whose gospel is their maw.

Such then was Milton's poetry, the poetry of one essentially an artist, one of whom it was soon found "that whether aught was proposed me by them that had the overlooking, or betaken of mine own choice, in English or other tongue, prosing or versing, but chiefly this latter, the style by certain vital signs it had was likely to live". Then had come, as I have tried to describe, the conviction that he had a burden to bear, a message to deliver, a poem to write which was to be "an elaborate song to generations" celebrating the great work done for the Church and People of England, a reform of reformation. There followed the long and bitter process of disillusionment, the final result of which was the abandonment of the thought of an historical poem (except so far as he might persuade himself that this had been achieved in the two *Defensiones*), and what took its place was an indictment of human weakness, and that not as the expression of an intuitive, passionate conviction but as the fruit of experience and the quite conscious reflection on that experience. Can *Paradise Lost* or *Paradise Regained* or—and this will need some special consideration—*Samson*

Agonistes be reckoned as prophetic poetry? Of intuitive, prophetic poetry the characteristic is this—and the same is characteristic of prose like that of Burke at his greatest moments and of Carlyle—that style and thought are inseparable, that these poets and orators write most imaginatively when their thought is at once profound and passionate. Is it so with these poems of Milton? Is it the message that remains with us when we have finished the poem and the beauty of the passages where this message is propounded, as it is with (say) *The Prelude*, or is it the story just as such, the characters, and the art with which these are presented, the beauties of diction and imagery and verse?

There are difficulties in coming to a final and detached judgement as to wherein lies the value of *Paradise Lost*. We have for some years now been passing through such a radical change of perspective that it is difficult to estimate the poem quite fairly, to detach our minds in reading from our traditional interest in the matter, whether we are in sympathy or out of sympathy with that tradition. The poem has no longer for us the appeal it possessed for those who saw in it, as the Greeks saw in the *Iliad*, a chapter of history. Yet we are not so far rid of that feeling that we can contemplate it without some disposition to challenge the theological positions, its central justification of God's ways to men. That Milton recognises that some justification is needed, and therefore lays such stress on Man's complete freedom, is something, and distinguishes Milton from his Calvinist contemporaries, like Baxter and Bunyan. But the Calvinist could take refuge in the mystery, the inscrut-

ableness of God's Will. It was altogether Milton's way
to insist on finding an intelligible, a reasonable justification. But the defence is too purely legal. Adam, created
free, and forewarned of what may threaten his welfare,
chose, influenced by his love for Eve, to disobey an
arbitrary command, a tabu, and thereby entailed on all
his unhappy posterity guilt, and a depraved will which
led only too easily to fresh falls and the continuous de-
generation of mankind. God, indeed, by the death of
His Son has relieved those who accept that Atonement
of their inherited guilt, and by His Grace helps those
who strive to recover their freedom and render God the
service due to Him. But those who accept are few and
never will be many. Such a justification is quite a different thing from Pope's attempt to "vindicate God's
ways to Man." Milton's defence of God's condemnation
of the whole race in Adam in the *De Doctrina* is rather
on the lines of Butler's *Analogy*. This entailing of the
sin of the parents on the children is in line with the way
God works:

It is however a principle uniformly acted on in the divine proceedings, and recognised by all nations and under all religions from
the earliest period, that the penalty incurred by the violation of
things sacred (and such was the Tree of Knowledge of Good and
Evil) attaches not only to the criminal himself but to the whole
of his posterity. It was thus in the Deluge etc....God declares
this to be the method of his justice...visiting the iniquity of
the fathers upon the children unto the third and fourth generation
of them that hate me, etc., etc.

It is a little strange to hear Milton speaking of the tree
as a holy thing, in view of his general refusal to recognise holiness in things at all. Is he not here confounding

the holiness of principles, of justice, etc. and the sacredness of tabus, the breach of which entails mischief on good
and bad alike? These and similar things in *Paradise Lost*
pressed heavily on my generation (and do so on readers of
to-day to some extent), insomuch that we were not able
to read the poem as we read Homer and Virgil without
troubling ourselves about the theology any more than
we do about the quarrels of the gods and the anger of
Juno. For the poem is a Christian poem. If Mr Tillyard feels that Milton's great poem is pessimistic, and
attributes this tone to the failure of the poet's high
hopes, it is necessary to remember that the pessimism,
so far as it is made explicit, is inherent in the Evangelical
Christianity of Milton's age and of later Evangelicalism,
indeed is inherent in Christianity in any form that is
historical: "Many are called but few are chosen." The
great scheme of salvation will benefit *only* the few, the
Elect; and if with Milton we are free-willers, yet it is
only the Heroic who will win through. For, before
coming to my main theme of the character of Milton's
poetry in these later works, I should like for a moment
to insist on the Christian character of the poem in all
its explicitly stated doctrines. Milton's lesson is not
contained in any new reading of Christian theology.
Paradise Lost is not a theological poem in the measure in
which Dante's is. This has been a little obscured of late
by the interest awakened by M. Saurat's study of the
De Doctrina. But if one is to understand how the poem
was welcomed by Protestant Christianity from Ellwood,
Addison, and others to Cowper, Foster, and the nine-
teenth-century Evangelicals, one must recognise that

all the main and prominent doctrines of the poem are
those of Evangelical Protestantism, unless we are to
make the Calvinist doctrine of determinism a cardinal
doctrine of all Protestantism, which I do not think it is.
For this is the only doctrine which the poem expressly
rejects, and it was rejected by the Quakers and by the
Wesleyans at the outset. Everything else is in the poem
—the Fall (through man's own free will); the corruption (though not the *complete* corruption) of man's will
through the Fall; the Atonement through the Death of
Christ; the renewal of man's will through the Spirit, the
Grace of God. Even Milton's Arianism, which is fully
developed in the *De Doctrina*, is not so clearly adum-
brated in the poem as has been stated by more than one
critic, misled by Milton's phraseology in the fifth book:

> This day have I begot whom I declare
> My only Son.

That points at first sight to the "generation" of the Son
at a period subsequent to the creation of the angels, including Satan and those who fell. Yet a little later in the
poem Abdiel "the dreadless angel" speaks of Christ
as he:
　　　　　　　　　　　　　　　by whom

> As by his Word the almighty Father made
> All things, even thee, and all the spirits of heav'n
> By him created in their bright degrees.

Satan disputes this:
　　　　　　　　　　　strange point and new!

> Doctrine which we would know whence learnt: who saw
> When this creation was? remember'st thou
> Thy making, while the Maker gave thee being?
> We know no time when we were not as now;
> Know none before us, self-begot, self-rais'd.

Surely it would have completed Satan's argument to
point out that Christ was this day begot, so could not
have been present at the first creation of those who have
just heard the proclamation. Clearly it is not the *generation* of the Son which has aroused Satan's anger. In
what sense Milton uses the word "begot" he has ex-
plained in the *De Doctrina*: "the Father is said to have
begotten the Son in a double sense, the one literal with
reference to the production of the Son, the other metaphorically with reference to his *exaltation*." Milton
expressly refers the text in the Epistle to the Hebrews,
i. 5 ("for unto which of the angels said he at any time,
Thou art my Son, this day have I begotten thee?"), to
the "exaltation of the Son above the angels". It is to
this "exaltation" that Raphael refers in the scene with
which the poem chronologically begins, and it is this
against which Satan rebels. If I might apply Milton's
distinction in my own way, when Hadrian declared
Titus Antoninus Pius his "son and successor" (Gibbon)
that day he "begot" him, metaphorically generated a
new thing, a prince.[1]

If *Paradise Lost* (and even *Paradise Regained*) seems
to many people to-day imperfectly Christian in spirit,

[1] Bishop Newton had not seen the *De Doctrina*, but he had no difficulty in understanding Milton's words and makes no charge of Arianism:
"We observed before that Milton was cautious what sentiments and
language he ascribed to the Almighty, and generally confined himself to
the phrases and expressions of Scripture; and in this particular speech the
reader will easily remark how much of it is copy'd from holy Writ by
comparing it with the following texts. I have set my Anointed upon my
holy hill of Sion; I will declare the decree. The Lord hath said unto me,
Thou art my son, this day have I begotten thee. Psal. ii. 6, 7....At the
name of Jesus every knee shall bow, of things in Heaven—and every
tongue shall confess that Jesus Christ is Lord, to the glory of God the
Father. Phil. ii. 10, 11."

it is not because of any explicitly heretical doctrines the poem gives expression to, such as Arianism, but because Milton's scale of values is not that of the orthodox and sincere Christian, Evangelical or Catholic. Take two of the doctrines, the Atonement and the doctrine of Divine Grace. It is not accurate to say, with some critics, that Milton ignores the atoning death of Christ in his *Paradise Regained* and makes the Temptation the great atonement. The Temptation is expressly declared to be preparatory to the death:

> But first I mean
> To exercise him in the wilderness,
> There he shall first lay down the rudiments
> Of his great warfare, ere I send him forth
> To conquer Sin and Death the two grand foes,
> By humiliation and strong sufferance.

Nevertheless, the thought of Christ's atoning death does not move Milton in the same passionate way as it moves the Evangelical poet of

> There is a fountain fill'd with blood
> Drawn from Emmanuel's veins;

or the Catholic Crashaw:

> Jesu no more, it is full tide
> From thy head and from thy feet,
> From thy hands and from thy side
> All the purple rivers meet.
>
> .   .   .   .   .   .
>
> This thy blood's deluge, a dire chance
> Dear Lord to thee, to us is found
> A deluge of deliverance;
> A deluge least we should be drown'd.

I suspect that Milton had seen much of this emotional religion and come to believe that it was a source of weakness as well as of strength, made for a self-centred regard for personal salvation rather than such a reform of Church and State as he longed for. At any rate to him the Atonement appears as a legal transaction, once carried through, by which the debt incurred by Adam had been paid and man set free again to serve God by the right use of his will.

In his treatment of the doctrine of God's prevenient grace there seems to me to be the same difference between his express recognition of the doctrine and the value which he attaches to it. To recover the full freedom forfeited by the Fall man needs the grace of God:

> Thus they in lowliest plight repentant stood
> Praying, for from the Mercy-seat above
> Prevenient grace descending had remov'd
> The stony from their hearts, and made new flesh
> Regenerate grow instead.

But as a fact he seems to lay small stress on grace as communicated directly or through the mediation of sacraments. Man's will is free, and on himself it depends whether tempted he falls like Adam, or overcomes every temptation like Christ, or falling repents and sincerely repenting recovers his freedom like Samson. Man is free and thereby responsible for what happens to him in this world and the next—that is the whole burden of the final message in these closing poems. It is the note which runs through the *De Doctrina*. It makes Milton on the very threshold of that work reject the doctrine of predestination; it makes him later reject the doctrine of the complete corruption of the human will, according to which without God's grace man cannot even desire to be saved; and when Milton comes to the doctrine which at once agitated and comforted so many, Bunyan, e.g., the question of the perseverance of the saints, while accepting the doctrine he insists on the necessity of the co-operation of the believer:

The final perseverance of the saints is the gift of God's preserving power, whereby they who are foreknown, elect, and born again, and sealed by the Holy Spirit, persevere to the end in the Faith and Grace of God, and never entirely fall away through any power or malice of the Devil or the World, *so long as nothing is wanting on their own part, and they continue to the utmost in the maintenance of faith and love.*

A doctrine that made the final issue so dependent on the human will would have left Bunyan a prey to the doubts and fears with which he fought such a battle in *Grace Abounding to the Chief of Sinners.* But it was the beginning and the end of the lesson that Milton had to proclaim in the great poem he had so long contemplated.

This narrowing of Milton's final message, this displacement of Christian values from the Atonement to the Temptation, accounts for the different temperament of his poem when compared with that of Dante, to say nothing of such lesser poets as Vondel or Crashaw. For it is around the doctrines of the Atonement by the Death of Christ and of Grace conferred in the Sacraments, especially the Eucharist, that the most intense feeling has centred in Christian poetry, Evangelical and Catholic. Dante can boldly declare that Hell, the City of Woe, is the work of Love:

> Giustizia mosse il mio alto fattore:
>   Fecemi la divina potestate,
> La somma sapienza e il primo amore,

and as we mount the steps of the *Purgatorio* and enter
the Earthly Paradise and as we ascend the circle of
Paradiso it is the fire and light of Love which illumines
and warms the whole, so that the effect of the early
cantos seems to fade from the memory, to be subsumed
in an entire Faith in

> L'Amore che muove il sole e l'altre stelle.

In Milton's cosmology Heaven is the coldest region,
especially when "God the Father turns a school-
divine", and states in stern and cold language the
justification of His ways to men. Yet there is beauty,
dignity and feeling in the speech of Christ when He
takes upon Himself the cost of redemption:

> Father, thy word is past, man shall find grace, etc.,

and in the fine lines which describe the reception of His
words by the assembled angels:

> No sooner had the Almighty ceas'd, etc.

Yet it all wants something, and the same want may be
felt by another approach. It was a favourite discussion
among the early critics, who was the Hero of Milton's
poem? Dryden, assuming that it must be Adam that
Milton intended, complains that Satan "foiled the
knight and drove him out of his stronghold to wander
through the world with his lady errant". That is a
characteristically flippant comment, and Addison was
surely right in saying that if the reader "will needs fix
the name of an hero upon any person in the poem it is
certainly the Messiah who is the hero, both in the
principal action and in the chief episodes", for surely

in an epic of Man's Fall and Redemption the Messiah ought to be the hero; and so Milton admits, for in the end Adam acknowledges that even his Fall is to be valued as the *occasion* of Christ's goodness:

> O goodness infinite, goodness immense!
> That all this good of evil shall produce,
> And evil turn to good; more wonderful
> Than that by which creation first brought forth
> Light out of darkness! Full of doubt I stand,
> Whether I should repent me now of sin
> By me done and occasion'd, or rejoice
> Much more, that much more good thereof shall spring,
> To God more glory, more good-will to Men
> From God, and over wrath grace shall abound.

Could anything be a more completely orthodox acceptance of the Christian philosophy of life? It is the sentiment expressed with a characteristic difference in the Middle English lyric:

> Adam lay ibounden,
>   Bounden in a bond,
> Four thousand winter
>   Thoght he not too long;
> And all was for an appel,
>   An appel that he tok,
> As clerkes finden writen in a boke.
>   Ne hadde the appel take ben,
>   The appel take ben,
> Ne hadde never our Lady
>   A ben heven Quene.
> Blessed be the time
>   That appel take was.
> Therefore we moun singen
>   DEO GRACIAS.

Yet that is not quite the effect which Milton achieves; perhaps it was impossible. We remember less Christ the promised redeemer than Christ who goes forth in all the panoply of Ezekiel's vision to overthrow the rebellious angels. Perhaps if Milton had read the greater prophets aright, and not like most Protestants of his day been more interested in the apocalyptic forecasts of "the two handed engine at the door", he might have found a better conception or produced a more Christian impression. His main thesis is that of the great Hebrew prophets, it is on Israel's *will* that all depends. God *will* save if they *will obey*:

Come now, and let us reason together, saith the Lord: though your sins be as scarlet, they shall be as white as snow; though they be red like crimson, they shall be as wool. If ye be willing and obedient, ye shall eat the good of the land: but if ye refuse and rebel, ye shall be devoured with the sword: for the mouth of the Lord hath spoken it.

Disobedient as the people are, God is ever yearning over them, crying to his people to repent:

Return, thou backsliding Israel, saith the Lord; I will not look in anger upon you: for I am merciful, saith the Lord, I will not keep anger for ever. Only acknowledge thine iniquity, that thou hast transgressed against the Lord thy God, and hast scattered thy ways to the strangers...and ye have not obeyed my voice.

God's love for Israel is the ever-recurring note:

"When Israel was a child, then I loved him, and called my son out of Egypt.... How shall I give thee up, Ephraim? how shall I deliver thee, Israel?... Mine heart is turned within me, my compassions are kindled together. I will not execute the fierceness of mine anger, I will not return to destroy Ephraim; for I am

God and not man, the Holy One in the midst of thee.... O
Israel, return unto the Lord thy God; for thou hast fallen by thine
iniquity... for the ways of the Lord are right, and the just shall
walk in them; but transgressors shall fall therein." "I will heal
their backsliding, I will love them freely: for mine anger is
turned away from him. I will be as the dew unto Israel: he shall
blossom as the lily, and cast forth his roots as Lebanon." "The
Lord appeared of old unto me, saying, Yea, I have loved thee
with an everlasting love: therefore with lovingkindness have I
drawn thee, etc."

Compared with the tone of these, at times so fierce,
prophets and poets, how cold is Milton's Deity who
greets only with scorn the first tidings of the rebellion
of Satan:

> And smiling to his only son thus said:
> Son thou in whom my glory I behold
> In full resplendence, Heir of all my might,
> Nearly it now concerns us to be sure
> Of our omnipotence, etc.

So sarcastically speaks the "Eternal eye". It could not
be otherwise. Milton's God must be the God of scientific theology. Greek philosophy taken up by Christian
theology had for the God of the Hebrew prophets, so
transcendent yet so human, substituted a God who is
a being without parts or passions, pure being, the Idea
of Good, the First Mover, and what could poetry do
with it except in such a momentary vision as Dante
adumbrates at the end of the *Paradiso*?

But leaving these preliminary considerations, let us
look broadly at the poem as an epic, a narrative poem.
Is there anything greater, more sublime, than the first

four books, with one qualification to which I shall
come? In these books one "stroke", as Addison would
call it, of creative and surprising genius follows another
—Satan and the angels prostrate on the floor of Hell,
Satan's dialogue with Beelzebub, his progress across
the burning marle:

> the torrid clime
> Smote on him sore besides, vaulted with fire;
> Nathless he so endured;

the rousing of the angels, and that tremendous "stroke"
which one might hardly have expected from Milton,
Satan shaken with remorse as he surveys the fallen
followers of his pride:

> Thrice he assay'd, and thrice in spite of scorn
> Tears such as angels weep burst forth; at last
> Words interwove with sighs found out their way.

Is there even in Shakespeare a greater moment? And
Shakespeare might have marred it by a touch of bom-
bast or wit. Then there are the devils themselves treated
as the gods of idolatry, into whose description Milton
pours all the Biblical hatred of the gods of the peoples
surrounding Israel and their worshippers; and that
leads on to Pandemonium, a trifle fantastic, it seems to
me, but preparing for the great debate in Hell. And in
the midst of these dramatic and picturesque scenes
comes a passage of pure poetry, poetry that makes you
forget the story, spell-bound by the loveliness of the lines:

> Anon they move
> In perfect phalanx to the Dorian mood
> Of flutes and soft recorders; such as rais'd

> To higth of noblest temper Heroes old
> Arming to battle, and in stead of rage
> Deliberate valour breath'd, firm and unmov'd
> With dread of death to flight or foul retreat,
> Nor wanting power to mitigate and swage
> With solemn touches, troubled thoughts and chase
> Anguish and doubt and fear and sorrow and pain
> From mortal or immortal minds.

The second book is full of great "things" (to use Saintsbury's favourite phrase), the debate, Satan's heroic choice of the exploration of Hell and Chaos, his encounter with Sin and Death:

> on the other side
> Incens't with indignation Satan stood
> Unterrifi'd, and like a Comet burn'd
> That fires the length of Ophiucus huge
> In th'Artick sky, and from his horrid hair
> Shakes pestilence and war;

the description of Hell in classical manner with such Miltonic touches as that of the angels deep in philosophic discourse

> Of Providence, Foreknowledge, Will, and Fate,
> Fixt Fate, free will, foreknowledge absolute,
> And found no end in wandering mazes lost,

as though they were themselves so many Miltons contemplating a treatise *De Doctrina*. With the third book difficulties begin, when we are introduced to the other camp, the opponents of Satan, God, the Son and the angels. I am trying, of course, to look at the poem without the traditional associations which made Johnson shrink from criticising even Milton's presentation of the divine: "The characters of *Paradise Lost* which admit of examination are those of angels and men; of angels good and evil; of man in his innocent and sinful state." If Milton had been Homer (and there is in him more of Homer than of either Virgil or Dante, so little is he of a philosophical poet) his gods would have been somewhat better characters than their Titanic oppoents, certainly more strong and beautiful:

> 'tis the eternal law
> That first in beauty should be first in might,

as Keats, in the spirit of the Greeks, declares. But Milton was in a difficulty. His God was twofold, the God of the Bible and the Deity of Philosophy as taken up into Christian theology. How is he to deal in an epic poem modelled on Homer and Virgil with such a transcendent conception? A Dutch critic, comparing Milton's poem with Vondel's drama, finds that one advantage of the epic form is that it allowed the poet to introduce the Deity on the stage of the action.[1] It is a doubtful advantage. Dante, the great theological poet, wisely abstains from any personal intervention of God or Christ. The closing vision is a theological dogma made, as it were, sensible—Plato's idea of the good, source at once of being and knowledge, revealed as the Trinity and

---

[1] "Vondel's *Lucifer*, the stage for which is situated in Heaven, suffers in the most palpable fashion from the complete inactivity of the person of God. God certainly sends out messengers and commands, but He Himself stands outside the action. One wishes, one expects, to see Him enter, or at least to hear His voice." (Nicolaus Beets.) In fact he behaves as perhaps President Wilson should have done during the negotiation of the Versailles Treaty, remained on Mount Sinai and occasionally lightened and thundered when things were not going right, when any of the fourteen points was being forgotten.

revealing within itself the Incarnation of the Second
Person:

> In that exalted lustre's deep, clear ground
>   methought that I beheld three circles glow
>   of threefold hue, in one dimension bound;
> One by the other seemed as bow by bow
>   reflected, and the third was like a flame
>   which equally from either seemed to flow.
>
> .   .   .   .
>
> That circle which appeared in Thee endued
>   with a reflected radiance, when I turned
>   to scan awhile its shape and magnitude,
> Of that same hue with which it inly burned
>   seemed painted in the likeness of a man;
>   to solve which wonder my whole spirit yearned.[1]

That is metaphysical poetry, metaphysical and mystical,
as Milton's never is. Milton's mind was neither mystical
nor metaphysical. In the *De Doctrina* and in the poem,
when Milton argues or states principles, his method is
that of a lawyer, accumulating texts to establish each
position. And the consequence of bringing in God the
Father, as a School Divine or a General planning a
campaign, is that all sense of mystery is taken from
Milton's exposition of the Pauline theology of the Fall
and the Redemption. If Milton, as I have said, could
have left out theology and drawn direct from the Bible
the impression conveyed by the greater prophets, the
vision of Isaiah who saw God seated amidst the cheru-
bim, a God who denounces sin and yet yearns over His
children, and had he combined this with something of

[1] Dante's *Paradiso*, tr. G. Bickersteth: a wonderful translation of
the poem.

the spirit of the Gospels, the thought of God as a
Father, he might have achieved in poetry what he aimed
at in the *De Doctrina*, an escape from the subtleties of
theology to the simpler, more concrete presentation of a
God transcendent and yet intensely human, a God who
claims affection as well as obedience.

Milton does indeed take the Scriptures as his chief
guide in portraying God,[1] but like all the great Protestant
Reformers he misplaced the values, laying stress, in the
Old Testament, on the historical books and the apocalyptic element in the later parts of the Book of Daniel,
and in the New Testament on the Book of Revelation,
while in the New Testament more generally the argumentative Epistles overshadowed the revelation of
Christ in the Gospels.

One is made so much aware in these first books of
great spaces and great forces, the dauntless might of
Satan, the infinite extent of the Universe, as Milton
has learned to conceive of it in his imagination,[2] so

---

[1] "If then the Scriptures be in themselves so perspicuous, and sufficient
of themselves 'to make men wise unto salvation' that 'the man of God
may be perfect, thoroughly furnished unto all good works', through
what infatuation is it that even the Protestant divines persist in darkening
the most momentous truths of religion by intricate metaphysical comments, on the plea that such explanation is necessary; stringing together
all the useless technicalities and empty distinctions of scholastic barbarism,
for the purpose of elucidating those Scriptures which they are continually
extolling as models of plainness? As if Scripture, which possesses in itself
the clearest light, and is sufficient for its own explanation, especially in
matters of faith and holiness, required to have the simplicity of its divine
truths more fully developed, and placed in a more distinct view, by
illustrations from the abstrusest of human sciences, falsely so called." *De
Doctrina,* i. xxx. *De Scriptura Sacra.*

[2] In the seventh book especially, though to some extent throughout
the poem, Milton has come near to satisfying his early expressed intention of writing a cosmic as well as an historical poem; and if you will
read Miss Marjorie Nicolson's interesting paper, "Milton and the

fond of the illimitable and yet so definite in what he describes or suggests, we have heard so much of power and space, that what we miss is the ethical, the spiritual, God's justice and mercy as well as His power. Nor is the defect quite made good by God's justification, His exoneration of Himself:

> They therefore, as to right-belonged,
> So were created, nor can justly accuse
> Thir Maker, or thir making, or thir Fate;
> As if Predestination over-rul'd
> Thir will, dispos'd by absolute Decree
> Or high foreknowledge; they themselves decreed
> Thir own revolt, not I etc.

True enough; and yet, to our feeble minds, not only Mercy of which God speaks but simple Justice would seem to require some consideration of the human nature given to Adam and Eve, its limitations, before such sweeping judgements were endorsed. Our feelings call for some redress, something to counterbalance this stern judgement, and this is to some extent supplied by the speeches of Christ, especially that in which He takes upon Himself the penalty of man:

> Father, thy word is past, man shall find grace:
> And shall not grace find means, that finds her way,
> The speediest of thy winged messengers,
> To visit all thy creatures, and to all

Telescope" (ELH, *A Journal of English Literary History*, April, 1935) you will see how the work of Galileo had expanded Milton's imagination. Nothing except the character of Satan in the first books is greater than Milton's management throughout the poem of the sense of infinite extent, a space that transcends all limits; and nothing in the poem has come nearer to anticipating the conclusions of modern science, or had a greater influence on later poetry, if Milton's blend of science and the Book of Genesis must still remain strange.

Comes unprevented, unimplor'd, unsought?
Happy for man so coming; he her aid
Can never seek, once dead in sins and lost:
Atonement for himself, or offering meet,
Indebted and undone, hath none to bring;
Behold mee then, mee for him, life for life
I offer, on mee let thine anger fall;
Account mee man; I for his sake will leave
Thy bosom, and this glory next to thee
Freely put off, and for him lastly die
Well-pleas'd, on mee let Death wreck all his rage.

To some extent but not entirely. Christ does not become sufficiently the central figure of the poem. He is seen more vividly later in his anger and might. Milton is more himself, at ease in the conduct of his story, when, this scene over to the music of the angels' hymns, we are brought back to Satan voyaging across "the Backside" of the created Universe, and the poet is free to pour scorn upon what, from the outset, he had hated as the gates of Hell—the magical element in religion, the deluded mortals who hope to sneak into Heaven by donning the garb of a monk:

they who, to be sure of Paradise,
Dying put on the weeds of Dominic,
Or in Franciscan thought to pass disguis'd.

To what then do we owe the unequalled greatness of these opening books? Mr Tillyard is disposed to attribute their buoyancy and ample breath to the probable fact that they were composed in the same mood, perhaps at the same time, as the *Defensio Secunda* of 1654, before the final cloud of disillusionment had begun to settle; that sense of disillusionment which Mr Tillyard finds

pervading all the last books. I think myself that their
quality is rather due to the freedom with which, in this
part of the story, Milton's imagination and invention
could work, untrammelled by Biblical or Ecclesiastical
tradition. Everything is of his own creation. He works
here like his own Deity creating a new Heaven and Hell
and Earth and their inhabitants, unknown to any pre-
ceding theologian or poet; and his greatest creation,
Satan, is so dominating a figure that, as Shakespeare
with Mercutio in *Romeo and Juliet*, the poet has to
dismiss him from the stage before the poem reaches its
conclusion.

But another question faces us when we recall in
imagination the pageantry, and hear, recollecting in
tranquillity, the roll of its great harmonies. What is
it that is so great in these books? Is it the spiritual,
the prophetic element? Can we recall passages which
are of the same kind as those I have read from Isaiah,
of the same kind as made the late Lord Balfour say that
poems like *The Prelude* and others of Wordsworth are
not didactic poems but prophetic utterances; and the
same I would venture to say is true of Emily Brontë's
lines which I have already cited, of some of the short
poems of William Blake, of Emily Dickinson, and of
Edmund Burke on the social contract:

Society is indeed a contract. . . . Each contract of each particular
state is but a clause in the great primaeval contract of eternal
society, linking the lower with the higher natures, connecting
the visible with the invisible world, according to a fixed compact
sanctioned by the inviolable oath which holds all physical and all
moral natures in their appointed place:

or of some paragraphs of Carlyle's *Sartor Resartus*, as "Natural Supernaturalism"? These express intuitions, reasonings, the logic of which is untraceable, for the premisses lie too deeply hidden in the complexities and experiences of a feeling and seeing mind. It is not so, I think, with Milton. His justification of God's ways to men is didactic, not prophetic; and it is so throughout the poem. But didactic verse is never pure, unalloyed poetry. It may at times rise, as in Dryden and Pope, to the level of effective poetic oratory, poetic declamation. It never becomes poetry, pure and simple, till the didactic becomes merged in the prophetic, till you feel that the poet is not expounding or defending a thesis but pouring forth in imaginative language and moving rhythms the intuitive images which rise from the unanalysable blend of sense, emotion, and thought. *The Prelude* abounds in passages of dull or awkward narrative and reflection. The poet emerges when a skating experience, the vision of a mountain raising its head suddenly seen from a stolen boat, a girl's dress tormented by the wind, becomes a mystical, imaginative, spiritual experience. It is the intuitive, the *prophetic* element which gives life and power to Wordsworth's poem. What is great in *Paradise Lost* is *the art*, the creation of great scenes and characters and incidents, that and the style and verse, a style that it is idle to censure because others have used it for inappropriate subjects. Into the telling of his story Milton throws himself as passionately as Wordsworth, but not in the same way, not intuitively recording the voice, as it were, of some inner revelation but argumentatively, e.g. in the scenes between Satan and

Abdiel; and these passages are not always well sustained. They can become, as in the account of angelic loves and digestion, a little flat, even a trifle absurd.

But to return to my survey of the poem. You may say that Milton had the same freedom of imagination and invention in describing the wars in heaven, the theme of the fifth and sixth books. But here the poet is faced with a difficulty, or a twofold difficulty, one of which recurs on the temptation of Adam and Eve. Why does Satan rebel, and why is he followed by "the third part of Heaven's host"? If the third part of a school or college or nation broke into rebellion we should be driven, or strongly disposed, to suspect some mismanagement by the supreme powers, otherwise, as Mr Gladstone complained the English people did when judging of the Irish, we must attribute to the rebels a double dose of original sin. But original sin was not yet conceived, unless we are to accept as literal what Satan later hears from his daughter and wife in Hell. Pride was the traditional motive for Satan's Fall, and Milton accepts that tradition and pitches on the Exaltation of the Son as the immediate efficient cause. But for Milton *all* sin was revolt against reason, and unfortunately neither for Satan nor later for Adam and Eve is it clear how they revolted against reason, for no reason is given either for the sudden and apparently capricious exaltation of the Son, nor later for the capricious prohibition of eating of the fruit of the Knowledge of Good and Evil. Milton's conception of the action of reason in the field of conduct is too abstract. If reason is our guide in conduct it is reason, as William James argues, at work, either in ourselves individually, or in the social consciousness which mainly creates and supports our standards, at work on experience, so that men are in a process of learning what is good and right. But of Satan's experience before this crisis we know nothing except what is hinted at later in the speech of Sin, and that implies that Satan had already yielded to temptation. For him too a woman had been the misleader. Adam and Eve again have had little or no experience. "Aspiring above their orders" is what Milton in an early tract ascribes to both Satan and Adam; and this might have been made some use of, for you will remember that Piccarda in Dante's *Paradiso* claims that the blessed know nothing of discontent but rejoice in their relative positions:

> "But tell me ye who tarry here in bliss,
>   Would ye not fain ascend to regions higher,
>   To win more friends or to see more than this?"
> All smiled at first to hear me thus inquire:
>   Then with such radiant gladness she replied,
>   Methought her burning in love's primal fire:
> "Brother, our wills are wholly satisfied
>   By love, whose virtue makes us will alone
>   What we possess and thirst for nought beside."[1]

But there is no hint of the kind in *Paradise Lost*. What we gather is seemingly that the will of God, however arbitrary it may appear, is to be obeyed. *That* is reasonable. Heaven is a totalitarian state.

The second great difficulty is the thought of a War in Heaven as we have come to conceive of Heaven and

[1] Dante's *Paradiso*, tr. G. Bickersteth.

God. Had Milton's been a pagan theology, where gods may contend against gods, these books might have outshone the *Iliad*, for Milton was well qualified to describe great deeds of what Spenser calls "derring-do", and his sympathies were quickly kindled for a courageous rebel like Satan or a dauntless supporter of the truth against odds like Abdiel. Had he not himself been the Abdiel of a great cause matched against Salmasius and all the banded forces of scholarship and the reverence for kings:

> Servant of God, well done, well hast thou fought
> The better fight, who single hast maintained
> Against revolted multitudes the cause
> Of truth, in word mightier than they in arms.

But when it comes to the actual physical combat one feels that after all these are not Homeric combatants, men or gods, but angels contending with the Almighty; and the battle scenes become purely decorative, not enhanced by the invention of artillery and the interchange of jibes and jokes. Only when the Son sallies forth, the Second Omnipotence, do we recover a sense of the sublime. Here Milton makes that use of the Hebrew prophets which I would have had him do more often, and to finer, more spiritual issues, as he invests the Son with all the mysterious accessories of Ezekiel's vision of God:

>   forth rushed with whirlwind sound
> The chariot of paternal Deity,
> Flashing thick flames, wheel within wheel undrawn
> Itself instinct with spirit, but convoy'd

By four cherubic shapes, four faces each
Had wondrous, as with stars their bodies all
And wings were set with eyes, with eyes the wheels
Of Beril, and careering fires between;
Over their heads a crystal Firmament,
Whereon a Saphire throne, inlaid with pure
Amber, and colours of the showry Arch.

If there is a falling off of interest in the later books it
was inherent in the subject. Who could make an heroic
poem of the story of Adam and Eve tempted to trans-
gress a tabu? Milton has done his best in the ninth
book, the varied decorative material of which is all that
it could be. But it is not till the Fall is accomplished
that the two characters, and especially Eve, grow human
and winning. How natural are all the sequences of
feeling, their mutual reproaches, the awakening of
Adam to the prognostics of disaster,

O miserable of happy is this the end, etc.,

the repentance of Eve, her complete self-abandonment
in her love for Adam, the reconciliation, reminder of that
side in Milton's character which it is so easy to forget:

She ended weeping, and her lowly plight,
Immoveable till peace obtained from fault
Acknowledg'd and deplor'd, in Adam wrought
Commiseration; soon his heart relented
Towards her, his life so late and sole delight,
Now at his feet submissive in distress,
Creature so fair his reconcilement seeking,
His counsel whom she had displeas'd, his aid:
As one disarm'd, his anger all he lost,
And thus with peaceful words uprais'd her soon.

The least interesting part of the poem is doubtless the visions and narrative of the last books when Michael descends to continue the instruction of Adam which Raphael had begun before the disaster. This was an afterthought, for in the earlier planned drama the consequences of the Fall were to have been presented in a symbolic Masque. Yet even these books have their interest of vivid presentation and of Milton's passionate comment when his own religious sensibilities are quickened, his hatred of religious materialism, of magic, his dislike of priests, his vindication of love as the fulfilling of the law. For if the charge which Mr Eliot brings against Milton of having disturbed the "unified sensibility" of poetry as we find it in Donne and the "metaphysicals" is taken to mean that his feeling ever loses touch with what he is saying poetically, I should deny it, with some exceptions which I have touched on. Through all the poem, and not least these more expository later books, runs the same passionate conviction as we met with in the early tracts that Milton is defending what he believes to be the purely spiritual character of the Christian religion. And then comes the quiet close, condemned by Addison and Bentley, which I would use to modify somewhat Mr Tillyard's finding of an ultimate pessimism in the poem. I do not think that Milton himself ever despaired of the Good Cause. Even after the Restoration he was ready, when he thought he might speak with safety, to take the field again in the battle against Popery, in *Of True Religion etc.* 1673. On his own past he was yet to have a word to say in *Samson Agonistes.* The pessimism of *Paradise Lost* is the

pessimism inherent in Evangelical Christianity and the
Puritan outlook upon life. The decline of Puritanism,
says Gardiner,

> may be traced to many causes but above all to the growth of a con-
> viction that it exalted the few at the expense of the many. The
> highest aim of the Protectorate was the defence of the so-called
> people of God. The highest aim of Puritan literature was the
> exaltation of the strong at the expense of the weak—of the pre-
> eminently good at the expense of the moderately virtuous....
> Human nature took its revenge in politics and literature.

A great story—though one involving certain inherent
difficulties and certain others due to its relation to our
traditional faith—a great story vividly and feelingly
told, with a feeling that lives along the line from first to
last—what of the poetry? Here again there is at present,
grown stronger since the war, a determined revaluation.
Of the poetry of *Paradise Lost* Landor, who hated its
theology, had no doubt: "After I have been reading
Paradise Lost I can take up no other poet with satisfac-
tion. I seem to have left the music of Handel for the
music of the streets, or at best for drums and fifes".
"I recur to it incessantly as the noblest specimen in the
world of eloquence, harmony and genius." Of the
pregnancy of Milton's style Raleigh quotes an early
critic: "A reader of Milton must be always upon duty;
he is surrounded with sense; it rises in every line, every
word is to the purpose. There are no lazy intervals: all
has been considered, and demands and merits observation.... Milton's words are all substance and weight;
fewer would not have served his purpose, and more
would have been superfluous." That is not how Mr T. S.

Eliot, Mr Leavis, Mr Read, and perhaps Mr Dobree, speak about Milton's poetry as such to-day. They have all of late shown a tendency to contrast, in a depreciatory spirit, the poetic diction of Milton compared with that of Dryden. Milton, Mr Eliot contends, is of necessity at times prosaic, because he has elected a perch from which he cannot afford to fall. "Milton", says Mr Dobree, "made the language stiff and tortuous, even distorted, unusable in that form by other poets, as Keats was to discover, but Dryden made it miraculously flexible. Milton may be the greater poet of the two, but in this respect *he injured our poetry*, while Dryden conferred upon it the greatest possible benefit." Personally I have always disliked and distrusted this estimate of a poet by his influence upon others. In the first place the worth of a work of art is not thus relative. It is absolute, self-contained. In the second, these judgements are very hard to make good. It is so easy to attribute to the influence of one man what is due to a more general movement and influence. Dryden's felicitous use of a more conversational and easy debating hard-hitting diction was but one pre-eminent example of a more general phenomenon. Moreover, Dryden himself recognised that it was not entirely suitable for all themes. His own style, as Verrall pointed out, gained in strength from his reading of *Paradise Lost*; and when he came to write the *Fables* he too felt the need of a phrasing more remote from that of every day. If Keats discovered that he could not follow Milton continuously, it was after writing in the first *Hyperion* a fragment of singularly beautiful poetry. But the im-

portant thing to note is that if Keats resolved to change
the style of his poem, to move away from Milton in the
direction of Dante and Dryden—but the Miltonic
strain is by no means entirely eliminated in the second
version—it was because he meditated a rather different
kind of poem, instead of an epic on the diffuse model,
a metaphysical poem. For nothing is more idle than
to pass judgement on a poet's diction without strict
attention to the purpose the poet had in view, the tone
and atmosphere which it seemed to him the subject
required. For certain purposes, satire and discursive,
argumentative poems like the *Religio Laici*, etc., Dryden
undoubtedly did help to make the English language
more forcible and flexible. His argumentative poems
and passages are superior to Milton's, unless we remember that Dryden's discourses are those of men in
London coffee-houses, Milton's of angels in Heaven
or only recently in Hell—they had not yet lost all their
original brightness. Dryden's diction was, as I have
argued elsewhere, a development from the diction of
the metaphysicals. Technically, for the student of English poetic diction—if one might include under that
head also the evolution of the poem—Dryden is the
most interesting of Donne's disciples. As the century
drew to an end "men's minds and ears were disposed
to welcome a new tone, a new accent, neither that of
high song,

> passionate thoughts
> To their own music chanted,

nor of easy, careless, but often delightful talk and song
blended...but the accent of the orator, the political

orator of a constitutional country". But from the outset Milton's mind was attuned to a higher strain, whether he wrote in verse or prose, and for his transcendent theme he necessarily (as Spenser had for a different purpose, the evocation of the atmosphere of romance of olden days) had to write in a style that was not that of everyday conversation or of oratory. And if Milton at times seems to come down off his perch and moves awkwardly, like the albatross in Baudelaire's poem, Dryden too can jump about from perch to perch in a less awkward but more jaunty style. For to my mind the central defect of Dryden as a poet—and I have discussed its deeper significance elsewhere—is that his happy phrases, even clever scenes in his plays, exist, so to speak, for their own sake, are not, as Milton's are, contributions to the expression of the central mood which dominates the whole poem. Mr Eliot, for example, makes much of Dryden's happy phrase in *The State of Innocence*, Dryden's dramatisation of *Paradise Lost*, "all the sad variety of Hell". But consider it in its setting. Milton's Satan, looking round on his new abode, cries:

> Is this the region, this the soil, the clime,
> Said then the lost Archangel, this the seat
> That we must change for Heaven, this mournful gloom
> For that celestial light?

This Dryden renders:

> Is this the seat the conqueror has given?
> And this the climate we must change for Heaven?
> These regions and this realm my wars have got,
> This mournful empire is the loser's lot;
> In liquid burnings or in dry to dwell
> Is all the sad variety of Hell.

The whole tone is changed, is lowered. One would not be surprised if Dryden's Satan spoke next of the advisability of putting up his umbrella. The "sad variety of Hell", a happy phrase, but would it have been appropriate in the mouth of Milton's Satan? I think not. Of Milton's style Mr Leavis writes: "I have in mind Milton's habit of exploiting language as a kind of musical medium outside himself, as it were...there is no pressure in his verse, no suggestion of any complex and varying currents of feeling and sensation; the words have little substance or muscular quality." What "outside himself, as it were" means I cannot conjecture;[1] but I should be inclined to charge Dryden with exploit-

[1] Mr Eliot has, since this lecture was written, brought his criticism to a definite statement in a *Note* contributed to the volume of *Essays and Studies* (1935) edited by Mr Herbert Read. He makes clear what, I take it, Mr Leavis means by this criticism. Mr Eliot is of course a very thoughtful critic, to the present generation of young poets almost the Dryden of our day. I read his criticism with the greatest interest if at times it seems to me capricious, affected a little by the desire to run counter to accepted judgements, and somewhat pontifical in manner and tone. In the present instance, moreover, as a mere professor I feel I am ruled out by his appeal to a higher court, "the ablest poetical practitioners of my own time" of which he is the Master. Does not, by the way, "poetical practitioner" for "poet" savour a little of the evil effect of Milton against which he is protesting? If I may, however, state my own reaction to Mr Eliot's *Note* it is this, that *again* the style is judged and condemned without careful consideration of the effect which Milton was necessarily aiming at. It is on a level with Jonson's condemnation of Spenser that "he writ no language". So much is this so that it disguises what I think is true, viz. that Mr Eliot's dislike of Milton's style really flows from a dislike of the spirit and tone of Milton's poem, a feeling which I confess to sharing to no small extent. *Paradise Lost* is not (if it ever will be) so remote from us that we can read it, as we can the *Iliad*, discounting much in the temper of the poem, for to my mind there is much in the *Iliad* which, if taken out of Homer and offered me as a spirit of our own day, I detest—the temper and ideals of the warriors of Dahomey.[2] In his more detailed criticism I cannot feel that Mr Eliot is

[2] See *Iliad VI* II 55-60, 61-5

ing language for its own sake by his use of fine phrases
and lines and whole speeches without a due regard to
the theme and spirit of the whole poem. That there is
no complexity or pressure of feeling in Satan's address
to the Sun in the fourth book seems to me astounding.

---

quite just, and again because he ignores the purpose of this or that poem
he takes his examples from. Thus he condemns the lines in *L'Allegro*:

> "While the plowman, near at hand,
> Whistles o'er the furrow'd land, etc."—

lines that delight me—on the ground that "it is not a particular plowman,
milkmaid, and shepherd that Milton sees (as Wordsworth might see
them), etc." I contend that for his purpose and effect a particular plowman etc. is not needed, might be misleading. All that is required is the
name and one right epithet; it must be a right one. The rest the reader's
imagination conjures up for itself, adjusting the picture to his own particular experiences, which will be very different for one whose summer
scenes are those of America and one all whose scenery is apt to be Scottish.
It is just so that one summons up an evening scene from the details in the
first verse of Gray's *Elegy*. Now for Milton's purpose, to suggest cheerfulness, Milton's "Whistles" is entirely right, for it is the sounds that give
the final touch of cheerfulness which the loveliest scene wants, seems to
wait for, while silence prevails. To me one of the marvels of *Paradise Lost*
is the degree to which Milton has succeeded in combining the creation
of a new heaven and earth and hell for which he had no guiding tradition
to help him (as Dante had) with a sufficiency of definition in respect
of position, direction and even detail. To have attempted more must have
issued in failure. Nor, though I think Mr Eliot is justified in laying stress
on the predominance of auditory impressions in Milton's descriptions,
is it all the truth. Other senses are included. I would take two passages:

> "Meanwhile in utmost longitude, where Heav'n
> With earth and ocean meets, the setting sun
> Slowly descended, and with right aspect
> Against the eastern gate of Paradise
> Level'd his evening rays: it was a rock
> Of alablaster, pil'd up to the clouds,
> Conspicuous far, winding with one ascent
> Accessible from earth, one entrance high;
> The rest was craggy cliff, that overhung
> Still as it rose, impossible to climb.
> Betwixt these rocky pillars Gabriel sat
> Chief of the angelic guards, awaiting night;

Its sole rival is, what possibly suggested it, the speech of Claudius when he has fled from the play-scene and pours forth the agitation of his tormented conscience; and Milton's is the more impressive because of the loftier character of Satan as we already know him and his more terrible situation. Claudius remains the worm he has always been. But Mr Leavis may mean that there are not the passionate ratiocinative subtleties of Donne's songs and elegies. But surely these would have been out of place, and surely there may be more than one kind of good poetry.

> About him exercis'd Heroic Games
> The unarmed youth of Heav'n, but nigh at hand
> Celestial armoury, shields, helms, and spears
> Hung high with diamond flaming and with gold."   iv. 538–54.

>   "As when to them who sail
> Beyond the Cape of Hope, and now are past
> Mozambic, off at sea north-east winds blow
> Sabaean odours from the spicy shore
> Of Araby the blest, with such delay
> Well pleas'd they slack their course, and many a league
> Cheer'd with the grateful smell old ocean smiles."   iv. 159–65.

I will not attempt to follow Mr Eliot in his comparison of Milton with Henry James and James Joyce. Between works so different in purpose there seems to me no medium. Lastly, if one is to judge a poet by his influence on the eighteenth-century poets it will not do to overlook the effect of Shakespeare. He too can write passages of rhetoric in the sense which Mr Eliot seems to give to the word, passages in which one feels he is playing with language; but after all art is a kind of game, and he too had imitators of his faults. The "poetical practitioners" of the day are in some ways the best of critics, not in all. From them the new poets receive their first recognition. While Jeffrey and the critics looked askance at Wordsworth, Keats was learning from him. While the reviews and even Leigh Hunt could make nothing of Browning, for Rossetti he was a discovery. But necessarily they pass too sweeping judgements on poets from whose art, become a convention, they are struggling to emancipate themselves. No one would accept as final Wordsworth's judgement on Dryden and Pope or those of later poets on Tennyson.

Another charge (perhaps really included in the former) brought to-day against Milton is that he has broken the tradition of English poetic diction.

> The predominance in various forms of Milton, from Thomson through Gray, Cowper, and Akenside to Wordsworth and, although allied with Spenser, through Keats and Tennyson... must receive enough attention... to bring out the significance of what we have witnessed in our time: the reconstitution of the English poetic tradition by the reopening of communications with the seventeenth century of Shakespeare, Donne, Middleton, Tourneur and so on. (Leavis.)

This is a claim difficult to understand exactly. In his own age Donne was *not* regarded as a preserver of the English tradition but, by Drummond for example (as the late Professor W. P. Ker insisted), as an innovator. The tradition of English poetic diction as established by Chaucer had been renewed and enriched by Spenser under Italian and French influence, and it was from Spenser in great measure, as Mr Charles Crawford and others have shown, that the dramatists, like Marlowe and the early Shakespeare, developed the poetic style which took the place of the banality of earlier dramatic diction. "Spenser writ no language", said Ben Jonson, and he and Donne are regarded as rebels against the Petrarchan and Spenserian tradition in their use of a language "such as men do use". But the change of style, of diction, went with and was symptomatic of a change in spirit and theme. Spenser's diction had been, like Chatterton's and Morris's later, due to the wish to recapture the tone and atmosphere of the older romance. Donne began as a satirist, and a strain of satire runs

creates a diction of his own or uses one that has become
more or less conventional, confined to poetry, and a
diction which approximates as closely as may be to the
language of the age. Everything will depend on the
individual's use, for either tendency may be made use
of by good poets in a hundred different ways, and "every
single one of them be right" if it suits his theme and
the spirit in which he writes. Wordsworth had hardly
rebelled against the diction of Darwin and the later
disciples of Gray in odes, when Keats was beginning to
create an exotic diction of his own. Mr Yeats and
Mr Rudyard Kipling have both written in the language
of the age, to very different issues. Mr Eliot's diction
is far from being always unliterary:

> In which sad light a carvèd dolphin swam.
> Above the antique mantel was displayed
> As though a window gave upon the sylvan scene
> The change of Philomel, by the barbarous king
> So rudely forced; yet there the nightingale
> Filled all the desert with inviolable voice.

That Milton could have written in a different style had
he chosen or had he turned to satire I do not think any
student of his prose could question. Nothing is more
interesting than the difference between the imagery of
his pamphlets and that of *Paradise Lost*, the former
colloquial and vigorous to the verge of coarseness, the
latter classical and dignified though always touched
with the light of his imagination, and when required,
the fire of his passionate temper.

And Milton did write in another vein and style when
he turned, at the suggestion of Ellwood, to write *Paradise Regained*.

CHAPTER VI

'Paradise Regained' — Milton's Christ — 'Samson Agonistes'—Milton's final vindication of himself and those he followed in the great deeds of the Rebellion

WE are familiar with the story told by Ellwood, the Quaker, of the origin of *Paradise Regained*: "thou hast said much here of Paradise Lost; but what hast thou to say of Paradise Found?" Sir Walter Raleigh made delightful fun of the story on the just ground that *Paradise Lost* had already dealt with the theme inasmuch as the Atonement through the life and death of Christ is the main theme, the end of Michael's discourse. That is true; and yet, as I have suggested, it is what we learn from Milton's statements rather than are made to feel by the story. Ellwood felt, as we feel, some want, and Milton may have recognised this, or at any rate been glad to set over against the story of Adam's fall the steadfast resistance to temptation of the Second Adam. In doing so, moreover, he was completing the programme sketched in *The Reason of Church Government*. He had composed an epic on the "diffuse model" of Homer, Virgil and Tasso. He would now write one on the "brief model" of the Book of Job, a story told in dialogues between the tempter and the tempted, for Job's friends were also his tempters, his accusers. And for his purpose he felt the need of a style other than that of the longer poem, and he thought he had found it, for nothing can well be more different from the diction

and cadences of *Paradise Lost* than the restrained, severe
language of *Paradise Regained*.

But one thing Milton did not change, his reading of
human nature and history. His poem is not, as a poem
on the theme by Crashaw would have been, an ecstasy
over the love of Christ as revealed in his atoning death.
The atonement is, indeed, foreshadowed in the opening
speech of God the Father:

> But first I mean
> To exercise him in the Wilderness,
> There he shall first lay down the rudiments
> Of his great warfare, ere I send him forth
> To conquer Sin and Death the two grand foes,
> By humiliation and strong sufferance:
> His weakness shall o'ercome Satanic strength
> And all the world, and mass of sinful flesh;
> That all the Angels and Ætherial Powers,
> They now, and men hereafter may discern,
> From what consummate vertue I have chose
> This perfect Man, by merit call'd my Son,
> To earn Salvation for the Sons of men.

'Perfect Man."—Milton speaks like a Socinian, but
he is quite aware that this is he who has already in
Heaven been declared:

> By merit more than birthright Son of God,

and who has cast out Satan:

> him long of old
> Thou didst debel, and down from Heav'n cast
> With all his Army, now thou hast aveng'd
> Supplanted Adam, and by vanquishing
> Temptation, hast regain'd lost Paradise,
> And frustrated the conquest fraudulent.

It is in the Temptation that, by contrast with Adam, Christ shows himself perfect man. Milton's Christ is not quite the Christ of the Gospel of St John. He is drawn on the lines on which Milton had already sketched Cromwell in the hour of Cromwell's greatest ascendancy, one who had not, like Cromwell, *learned* to subdue "the whole host of hopes, fears, and passions which infest the soul", but has done so from his mother's womb, and is able to reject at once the temptations of sense, ambition and, if I, or Milton, understand aright the last temptation, the temptation to use miraculous power for self-glorification. *Paradise Regained* has been hardly judged, and Mr Belloc dismisses it with contempt. I must yet confess that, not greatly caring for the picture of the hero, and acknowledging the note of hardness which has crept more and more into Milton's temper, I cannot but enjoy and admire the serene power with which the lofty sentences are woven and the dignified rhythms move:

> The city which thou seest no other deem
> Than great and glorious Rome, Queen of the Earth
> So far renown'd, and with the spoils enricht
> Of Nations; there the Capitol thou seest
> Above the rest lifting his stately head
> On the Tarpeian rock, her Citadel
> Impregnable, and there Mount Palatine
> The imperial Palace, compass huge, and high
> The Structure, skill of noblest Architects,
> With gilded battlements, conspicuous far,
> Turrets and Terraces and glittering Spires—

and so on. There is more art in the drawing out of the

sense from line to line than a careless reader may at first perceive.

In *Paradise Lost* the poet and the prophet, or to put it otherwise, the poet as creator and the poet as critic, meet but fail to coalesce, come even into conflict with one another, leave on the reader's mind and imagination conflicting impressions. On the one hand the argument, as developed by Milton speaking in his own person or through the mouth of God (and Milton, as Professor Saurat has said, is the chief protagonist of Satan), aims at one effect, the justification of God's ways to men. The story itself, as the poet so vividly and dramatically presents it, leaves us with a very different impression, one not of entire acceptance of the justification. What do we see when we try to isolate the drama from the poet's contention? A war in heaven, aroused by the apparently arbitrary, almost capricious exaltation of one among many of the Sons of God; as a consequence, Satan's revenge by the seduction of Adam and Eve into a fatal breach of another apparently arbitrary tabu. If any moral springs straight out of the story itself it is, as I have said elsewhere, that the man must be the ruler in his own house:

> Therefore God's universal Law
> Gave to the man despotic power
> Over his female in due awe,
> Nor from that right to part an hour
> Smile she or lower.

In *Paradise Regained* there is less evidence of dualism, though even here, when Christ arraigns the whole of

Greek philosophy and poetry, it is difficult not to suspect
some inner conflict. But in the shorter epic the didactic
predominates. The interest centres less in the story and
characters than in the descriptions and dialogue.

With *Samson Agonistes* there is an abrupt and decisive
change of tone. In no poem since *Lycidas* have the poet
and the critic of life been so at one. In the early Elegy
the lament for King had been sustained throughout,
and twice lifted to the level of more passionate intensity:

> That strain I heard was of a higher mood,

by the poet's contemplation of his own experience, his
disappointments, and hopes, and fears. In similar manner Milton in this last drama turns back on himself and,
in a like strain of intense feeling, composes a dramatic
vindication of his own life, and of his action and that of
those whom he supported in the great historical crisis
through which he had lived, and the style and verse are
moulded to be the adequate investiture of his stern
theme. *Lycidas* and *Samson* are the most entirely sincere
and spontaneous of his quite serious poems, for
L'Allegro and *Il Penseroso* are delightful pastimes.

To realise this fully one must recall the treatment of
the story of Samson in Ecclesiastical Theology, and one
must note carefully what Aristotle calls the *dianoia*, the
sentiments of the poem in choral songs and in Samson's
speeches. Many critics have noted the more obvious
resemblances between Samson and Milton himself. He
too had wedded a wife from among the Philistines and
she had betrayed his fondest hopes. He too, as Masson
was the first to point out, had driven from the field a

boasting Harapha in the person of Salmasius. And now
he too was "fallen on evil days":

> Eyeless, in Gaza, at the Mill, with slaves,

left

> to the unjust tribunals, under change of times.

An *advocatus diaboli* might justly retort that Milton had
escaped the "unjust tribunals", and say with Dr Johnson, "no sooner is he safe than he finds himself in
danger, fallen on evil days and evil tongues and with
danger and with darkness compassed round". But one
will never be fair to Milton, supposing one wishes to be
so, if one thinks of him as complaining simply of his
own unhappy lot as a man. He is thinking of himself as
identified with "the Good Old Cause" which has gone
under. Thus, if even in the dramatic portrayal of
Samson's bitter repentance one seems to detect a personal touch, it is not because Milton has or thinks he
has anything to repent of so passionately in his own life.
It is a vicarious repentance of which Samson is the
mouthpiece. It is the English people, or those whom
God had chosen to do a great work, who have failed,
passed through the fire to perish in the smoke, laid
down their heads

> in the lascivious lap
> Of a deceitful concubine, who shore me
> Like a tame wether, all my precious fleece,
> Then turn'd me out ridiculous, despoil'd,
> Shav'n, and disarm'd among my enemies.

But the radical resemblance between Samson and Milton
is none of these things. To understand the significance
of the story for Milton one must, as I have said, recall

the reading of the story of Samson by, say, St Augustine and St Thomas Aquinas.

Two characters in Old Testament history caused considerable trouble to Christian moralists. They were Jephtha, who slew his own daughter,[1] and Samson, who committed suicide. "Praeterea, Samson, seipsum interfecit, qui tamen connumeratur inter sanctos (ut patet Hebr. xi). Ergo licitum est alicui occidere seipsum." So Aquinas puts the question (Quæst. 64, Art. 5, Obj. 4). In his answer he follows St Augustine, to whom the difficulty had been especially troublesome because he was busy combating the Roman and Stoical commendation of suicide. *Mors voluntaria* is, he contends, forbidden to Christians. What then of Samson? His answer is that Samson can only be excused on the ground that he acted under the direct inspiration and guidance of God. "Nec Samson aliter excusatur quod seipsum cum hostibus ruina domus oppressit, nisi quia Spiritus latenter hoc iusserat, qui per illum miracula faciebat"[2]; and when later he comes to consider the case of holy women who drowned themselves to escape violation he decides that they are to be excused only if they did so "non humanitus deceptae, sed divinitus iussae, sed oboedientes, sicut de Samsone aliud nobis fas non est cre-

---

[1] Milton has considered the story of Jephtha: "What greater good to man than that revealed rule, whereby God vouchsafes to shew us how he would be worshipt? and yet that, not rightly understood, became the cause that once a famous man in Israel could not but oblige his conscience to be the sacrificer, or if not, the jailor of his innocent and only daughter" (*The Doctrine and Discipline of Divorce*, 1642). See also my "A Note upon the *Samson Agonistes* of John Milton and *Samson of Heilige Wraeck*" ("Samson, or Holy Vengeance", by Joost van den Vondel, in *Mélanges Baldensperger*, Paris, H. Champion, 1930.)

[2] *De Civitate Dei.*

dere". We are bound by the Faith so to think about Samson. Donne, I may say in passing, rejects this doctrine.[1]

It is not of course Samson's suicide that is the interest of the story for Milton, though in the final Chorus he uses St Augustine's phrase *mors voluntaria* in disclaiming any such possible accusation. The main intention of the poem is emphasised in the Argument, which was doubtless the last thing written. Samson is required to play before the Lords and People:

he at first refuses, dismissing the publick Officer with absolute denyal to come; *at length perswaded inwardly that this was from God* he yields to go along with him, who came now the second time with great threatenings to fetch him; the chorus yet remaining on the place, Manoa returns full of joyful hope, to procure ere long his Son's deliverance: in the midst of which discourse an Ebrew comes in haste; confusedly at first and afterwards more distinctly relating the Catastrophe, what Samson had done to the Philistines, and *by accident* to himself; wherewith the Tragedy ends.

The interest for Milton is the thought of God as directly inspiring men by latent impulsion to do certain things which in normal morality are forbidden. He had already touched upon this in defending the execution of the King although it was clearly not the desire of the majority of the English people.[2] He is now to make it the justification of his own actions and those of the great men with whom he co-operated. God's right to

---

[1] John Donne, *Biathanatos*, III, 5, 4: St Augustine's view "hath no ground in history".

[2] Cromwell's election to power was "by the special direction of the Deity", "almost instructed by immediate inspiration" (*Defensio Secunda*).

exempt chosen individuals from moral prescripts is the
theme of the first choral song, the occasion being the
marriages of Samson:

> Just are the ways of God,
> And justifiable to men:
> Unless there be who think not God at all,
> If any be they walk obscure;
> For of such doctrine never was there School,
> But the heart of the fool,
> And no man therein Doctor but himself.
>   Yet more there be who doubt his ways not just,
> As to his own edicts found contradicting,
> Then give the reins to wandering thought,
> Regardless of his glory's diminution;
> Till by their own perplexities involv'd
> They ravel more, still less resolv'd,
> But never find self-satisfying solution.
> As if they would confine the interminable,
> And tie him to his own prescripts,
> Who made our laws to bind us, not himself,
> And *hath full right to exempt*
> *Whomso it pleases him by choice*
> *From national obstriction, without taint*
> *Of sin, or legal debt;*
> *For with his own laws he can best dispense.*

> .   .   .   .

> Down Reason then, at least vain reasonings down.

To this thought he will recur as he develops the action
of the play. It is a difficult kind of action to elaborate
dramatically, and to this is due in the main the defect
on which Johnson lays stress: "The play has a beginning and an end which Aristotle himself could not
disapprove; but it must be allowed to want a middle,

since nothing passes between the first act and the last that either hastens or delays the death of Samson". In this it does not differ greatly from such a play as the *Oedipus Coloneus*, which was probably in Milton's mind as he set forth the last day in the life of a great national hero. Moreover, how can an action which springs from the latent impulse of the spirit be developed with the clear logic of a drama by Racine? The Dutch poet Vondel attempted a play on the same theme, but he deprives the act of all dramatic conflict by making Samson learn in a dream exactly what he is to do and suffer.

"My locks", he tells the Chorus of Hebrew maidens, "are growing again. I am meditating vengeance on this heathen race, and that sooner than men suspect. The Spirit revealed to me this night a means to free myself from these bonds. Console yourselves! Weep no more! My departure is at hand. A triumphant death, wherewith the world shall ring, hangs over Samson's head. He shall not long, tormented and scorned by young and old, grind corn. They shall pay with the neck for the work I have done. This is my prayer, that after my death I be granted an obsequy, be buried in a grave of my fatherland."

The Chorus fears that he is meditating suicide, but he replies: "I swear to lay no hand upon my body; but I will, as becomes God's hero, give a glorious end to my life, an end that earth and sea shall talk of. You shall hear how the enemy came to *his* end". Vondel has to transfer the conflict of the drama to another theme, the legitimacy of drama on sacred subjects and in holy places. He had in mind the condemnation by the Amsterdam clergy of his own *Lucifer* (1654).

It is in a different manner that Milton's Samson
dimly apprehends the approaching end of life and
glimpses the possibility that he may yet be called on to
do some act of service to God. When the play opens we
see him repentant, admitting to the full that the fault is
his own. Whatever the Chorus may say or sing of the
mysteries of God's dealings with men, as is the manner
of Choruses in Greek drama, Samson is quite clear on
the fact that he is where he is because of his own con-
temptible weakness in yielding to his wife. It is a very
Miltonic repentance in which there is more of wounded
pride than of Christian repentance which includes for-
giveness. His fault, like Adam's, had been weakness:

> of what now I suffer
> She was not the prime cause, but I myself
> Who vanquish'd with a peal of words (O weakness)
> Gave up my fort of silence to a woman.

But weakness is no excuse:

> All wickedness is weakness; that plea therefore
> With God or man will gain thee no remission.

But aware of his sin, Samson is quite sure that God will
defend his own cause. When Manoah tells him of the
approaching feast and what is threatened and adds:

> So Dagon shall be magnifi'd, and God
> Beside whom is no God, compar'd with idols,
> Disglorifi'd, blasphem'd and had in scorn
> By th' idolatrous rout amidst their wine;
> Which to have come to pass by means of thee,
> Samson, of all thy sufferings think the heaviest,

Samson replies calmly:

> all the contest is now
> Twixt God and Dagon; Dagon hath presum'd,
> Me overthrown, to enter lists with God,
> His Deity comparing and preferring
> Before the God of Abraham. He, be sure,
> Will not connive or linger thus provok'd,
> But will arise and his great name assert;
> Dagon must stoop, and shall ere long receive
> Such a discomfit, as shall quite despoil him
> Of all these boasted trophies won on me,
> And with confusion blank his worshippers.

Manoah accepts these words, and Milton means us to do so, as prophetic. Nor will Samson admit reproof of his marriages. Here again he was acting under the inspiration of God. If his parents opposed the marriage they

> knew not
> That what I motioned was of God: I knew
> From intimate impulse, and therefore urged
> The marriage on.

Note the words "from intimate impulse", (spiritus latenter hoc jusserat) and his claim that his youth had been "full of divine instinct". He tells Harapha:

> I was no private, but a person rais'd
> With strength sufficient and command from Heaven
> To free my country.

When Harapha leaves he already feels that his death is certain, but that with it may come ruin to his foes:

> Yet so it may fall out, because thir end
> Is hate, not help to me, it may with mine
> Draw their own ruin who attempt the deed.

Commanded to appear Samson refuses at first, but while stating clearly the reasons which forbid him such a deed he adds:

> Yet that he may dispense with me or thee
> Present in temples at idolatrous rites
> For some important cause, thou needst not doubt.

And even before the officer returns he feels that God is leading him:

> Be of good courage, I begin to feel
> Some rousing motions in me which dispose
> To something extraordinary my thoughts.
> I with this messenger will go along,
> Nothing to do, be sure, that may dishonour
> Our Law, or stain my vow of Nazarite.
> If there be ought of presage in the mind,
> This day will be remarkable in my life,
> By some great act, or of my days the last.

Samson is still unaware of what that great act is to be, but feels that he is led by the Spirit. When, after the display of his strength, he is conducted to the pillar to rest:

> he stood as one who pray'd,
> Or some great matter in his mind revolv'd.

And then he saw what it was. The Chorus at once emphasises the thought which has guided Milton, the thought formulated by St Augustine. The death of Samson was not a case of *mors voluntaria* forbidden of God:

> O dearly bought revenge, yet glorious!
> Living or dying thou hast fulfill'd
> The work for which thou wast foretold
> To Israel, and now liest victorious
> Among thy slain *self-kill'd*

Not willingly, but tangl'd in the fold
Of dire necessity, whose law in death conjoin'd
Thee with thy slaughter'd foes in number more
Than all thy life had slain before.

So Milton reckons he is justified, and those whom he
supported in the great hour of vengeance, in the eyes of
God. Into no poem has he put more of his deepest
feeling, his own sufferings physical and mental (but
dramatised and so held at a distance), and those haunting
doubts about God's ways which had looked out even in
his early exultant prose: "O perfect and accomplish thy
glorious acts; for men may leave their work unfinished,
but thou art a God, thy nature is perfection: shouldst
thou bring us thus far onwards from Egypt to destroy
us in the Wilderness, though wee deserve, yet thy great
name would suffer in the rejoicing of thine enemies and
the deluded hope of all thy servants." So the Chorus
now in more despondent terms:

> God of our Fathers, what is man!
> That thou towards him with hand so various,
> Or might I say contrarious,
> Temper'st thy providence through his short course,
> Not evenly, as thou rul'st
> The Angelic orders and inferiour creatures mute,
> Irrational and brute, etc.

But in the end God vindicates himself and his servants.
That is Milton's faith. Others might waver or recant,
Pepys might feel much afraid that Mr Christian
"would have remembered the words that I said the day
the King was beheaded that were I to preach upon him

my text should be—*The memory of the wicked shall rot . . ..*" Not so Milton. "It was about this time", Bismarck said once in Sir Austen Chamberlain's presence, "that I reached that confidence in myself out of which a real belief in God's guidance of the world springs." So Milton had felt from the time he entered the fray. Wrongheaded he was perhaps, or as wicked as one may with Johnson or Mr Belloc choose to think him, but there is sublimity in this unwavering devotion to what he believes to be a great cause, the cause of truth and justice. He will not surrender that faith in truth and justice. It gives to his work, as to Dante's, a hue at times of malevolence, less dark than in the *Divina Commedia*, but the poems are sublime if "Sublimity is the echo of a great soul". It is this reflection of his own soul in the style and verse that makes criticism of faults seem idle. "The dignity, the sanity, . . . the just subordination of detail, the due adaptation of means to ends, the high respect of the craftsman for his craft and for himself, which ennoble Virgil and the great Greeks, are all to be found in Milton, and nowhere else in English literature are they all to be found." So A. E. Housman. But Milton's reaction to great political and religious crises is not the only possible one, and I should like to compare him in this respect with another poet.

CHAPTER VII

Wordsworth and the French Revolution— A contrast with Milton

IF we reflect on the possible experiences of a poet like Milton, Blake or Wordsworth, in passing through a revolution, a man of deep sensibilities, of active intellectual and imaginative reactions to the sensations and emotions which his temperament make so acute, and, finally, endowed with the power to express, to communicate to others, what he feels and thinks; if we reflect even in an *a priori* manner we can see different things which may happen, which the history of these poets and of others show us did actually happen. One thing is certain—the high hopes, the passionate agitations which the first movement of sympathy with a great effort to renew the life of a people arouses will be followed by an acute reaction, a profound sense of disillusionment. Every revolution, that is not a mere rebellion or *émeute*, seems to follow the same course, to arouse the same high hopes followed by the same reaction, disappointment turning to bitterness and a mutual hatred as intense as, and more fruitful in its frightful consequences than, the mutual goodwill of which the first stage had been so productive. Wordsworth saw it in France; we have seen it in our own days in Turkey, in Russia, and in Spain. Before he had himself been drawn into the movement, or meditated on the principles from which it proceeded and their significance,

Wordsworth was a sympathetic witness of the joy evoked in the hearts of Frenchmen far and wide; and not of Frenchmen alone:

> But Europe at that time was thrilled with joy,
> France standing on the top of golden hours,
> And human nature seeming born again.
>
>   A lonely pair
> Of strangers, till day closed, we sailed along,
> Clustered together with a merry crowd
> Of those emancipated, a blithe host
> Of travellers, chiefly delegates returning
> From the great spousals newly solemnized
> At their chief city, in the sight of Heaven.
> Like bees they swarmed, gaudy and gay as bees;
> Some vapoured in the unruliness of joy,
> And with their swords flourished as if to fight
> The saucy air. In this proud company
> We landed—took with them our evening meal,
> Guests welcome almost as the angels were
> To Abraham of old. The supper done,
> With flowing cups elate and happy thoughts
> We rose at signal given, and formed a ring
> And, hand in hand, danced round and round the board;
> All hearts were open, every tongue was loud
> With amity and glee.

"Amity and glee"—we know what succeeded, the fierce reaction, the powerful ebb, hatred and mutual suspicion succeeding to amity and glee—September Massacres—the "noyades"—the blood-bath. Little more than a year later Wordsworth, now an ardent revolutionary, sat in his upper room in a Paris hotel and, even in his mood of deeper sympathy with the principles of the Revolution, could not escape a sense of horror as he contemplated all that had happened:

> But that night
> I felt most deeply in what world I was,
> What ground I trod on, and what air I breathed.
> High was my room and lonely, near the roof
> Of a large mansion or hotel, a lodge
> That would have pleased me in more quiet times;
> Nor was it wholly without pleasure then.
> With unextinguished taper I kept watch,
> Reading at intervals; the fear gone by
> Pressed on me almost like a fear to come.
> I thought of those September massacres,
> Divided from me by one little month,
> Saw them and touched: the rest was conjured up
> From tragic fictions or true history,
> Remembrances and dim admonishments.
> The horse is taught his manage, and no star
> Of wildest course but treads back his own steps;
> For the spent hurricane the air provides
> As fierce a successor; the tide retreats
> But to return out of its hiding place
> In the great deep; all things have second birth;
> The earthquake is not satisfied at once;
> And in this way I wrought upon myself,
> Until I seemed to hear a voice that cried,
> To the whole city, "Sleep no more". The trance
> Fled with the voice to which it had given birth;
> But vainly comments of a calmer mind
> Promised soft peace and sweet forgetfulness.
> The place, all hushed and silent as it was,
> Appeared unfit for the repose of night,
> Defenceless as a wood where tigers roam.

That was Wordsworth's experience. Some readers

will remember with me the news from Constantinople when Abdul Hamid was displaced by the Young Turks, and when for a moment Mussulman and Christian, Turk, Greek, and Armenian were at one—for a moment, and then the reaction, a tyranny more cruel and cynical than even Abdul Hamid's; and later a massacre of the Armenians, compared with which the September Massacres are a small affair, the attempted annihilation of a people. Mr Walpole's description in his novel *The Secret City* is—eye-witnesses have assured me—entirely true of Petrograd, that picture of great crowds of people moving through the streets united by a vague but massive sense of emancipation, of mutual "amity and glee"; and we know there too what followed, in what a blood-bath the workers' republic was baptised, how there too a more savage and cynical tyranny succeeded the old. "Man's Inhumanity to Man makes countless Thousands mourn", and no sudden change of political conditions is going to cure at once so deep-seated a malady.

To this inevitable course of events, as I have said, poets as well as other men will react in different ways. One may through every disappointment of his first confident expectations remain a devoted adherent of the cause he has embraced, as passionate if more embittered, clinging to "the good old cause", attributing failure to the weakness and treachery of men and parties. Such was Hazlitt in the years which followed the French Revolution, clinging passionately to the cause of France even when Napoleon had become its representative, and seeing in the Battle of Waterloo only a miserable

triumph for the cause of reaction and petty monarchs
and tyrants; and Byron half shared his view, though an
aristocrat in temperament, whereas Hazlitt was a democratic child of English Nonconformity. Such too, as
we have seen, was Milton in the seventeenth century.
Steadily as the conflict deepened and men and parties
fell away he moved more and more towards "the left".
The Presbyterians in whose defence he had entered the
field of controversy became those who had gone to all
lengths and in the end turned tail, the object of his
bitterest contempt. In 1649 he became the champion
of regicide. He was not appalled by the massacres of
Drogheda and Tredah. For him Cromwell was our
"chief of men", though even Cromwell failed him
when he refused to make complete the severance of
Church and State, and when he dallied with the thought
of assuming the title of King. In truth Cromwell was,
compared with Milton, a conservative, his policy after
the Battle of Worcester—his "crowning mercy"—determined by nothing so much as the desire to secure
stability in the country, to substitute accepted authority
for the rule of the sword. When the Rump was restored
Milton could speak of Cromwell's rule, which he had
defended, as "a scandalous night of usurpation", and
when the whole nation was longing for the restoration
of Charles and an end of the rule of saints and major-
generals, Milton was still preaching republican doctrine and perpetual parliaments. During the remainder
of his life he sat apart, grimly contemplating the ruin
of his hopes, but still faithful to the cause, completing
his great poems of which the theme from first to last is

liberty, the freedom and responsibility of man, how Adam forfeited it by the greatest of all sins, weakness:

> All wickedness is weakness: that plea therefore
> With God or man will gain thee no remission.

How that liberty was restored:

> By one man's firm obedience fully tried
> Through all temptation.

How he who has fallen through weakness may yet recover his lost strength, and wreak vengeance on God's enemies, the mighty of the world.

But the effect *may* be different. It may induce a disbelief in the efficiency of political changes to achieve the true welfare of a people, of human nature, and the result may be a temper of stoicism, a readiness to say with Dr Johnson:

> How small of all that human hearts endure
> The part that laws or kings can cause or cure.

But such a type of mind is perhaps not likely ever to be exalted by revolutionary hopes. The man who has been carried away by these high ardours is more likely to react to a mood of cynical pessimism—Wordsworth has described such a character in *The Excursion*—unless he is saved by turning his mind, his beliefs and hopes in another direction, by discovering that man's happiness —or nine-tenths of his happiness—depends upon himself, flows from within, that it is there a revolution must be achieved, a turning round of the soul to behold the light, an inner illumination. This is what Blake found in his own strange way, passing through experiences the full history of which we cannot trace, but including what will seem to most of us an element of hallucination. This was the experience—in a somewhat more sober fashion—of Wordsworth, an experience described by himself in a poem which, however unequal, is one of the greatest in our language, *The Prelude*.[1]

Such an experience may, in Wordsworth's case did, beget a tendency to make too little of politics as a factor in human welfare, to become conservative and reactionary, for if it is true that the chief well-spring of human happiness is in a man's own soul, it is yet also true, as Plato taught, that the best of men cannot be entirely himself, must live a somewhat maimed and unhappy life, in an ill-ordered, ill-governed country. The intensity of Wordsworth's earlier emotional life left him exhausted in his later years; nor was Whig policy, in which reform and ruthless industrialism went hand in hand, of a kind to appeal to one who loved so well the open country-side, the free if exhausting labour of the peasant, who hated to see human beings treated as mere tools and not as individual souls, each a world to be saved.

What a profound and soul-stirring experience the

---

[1] Wordsworth states the antithesis in summing up the drift of *The Prelude*:

> For time had never been in which the throes
> And mighty hopes of Nations, and the stir
> And tumult of the world to me could yield,
> How far soe'er transported and possess'd,
> Full measure of content; but still I craved
> An intermixture of distinct regards
> And truths of individual sympathy
> Nearer ourselves.   XII. 112–19 (1805).

French Revolution was for Wordsworth when once his sympathies were awakened I need not detail. He has told the story twice, once in *The Prelude* in the first person, and again dramatically in the person of the Solitary in *The Excursion*. Facts which have come to light within recent years show us that the story in *The Prelude* is not after all complete, that some of the excesses hinted at in the story of the Solitary were committed by Wordsworth himself, that for a time he too had been one of those who deemed

> Old Freedom was old servitude, and they
> The wisest whose opinions stooped the least
> To known restraints.

That is, like Milton, like Blake, Wordsworth had felt that the emancipation of man was to extend not only to politics, to the state, but to sexual relations, to the family—that love was to be a law to itself. Of the young man, the seducer of Ruth, Wordsworth writes:

> The wind, the tempest roaring high,
> The tumult of a tropic sky,
> Might well be dangerous food
> For him, a youth to whom was given
> So much of earth, so much of heaven,
> And such impetuous blood.

The youth thus described is doubtless the young Wordsworth himself: but it was not tropical skies and storms that fired his blood, it was the strong air of a revolutionary epoch, an era of emancipation. It is I think a pity that a too timid regard for respectability kept the story of Wordsworth's passion for Annette Vallon so long hidden, as it was a misfortune that *The Prelude* itself remained unpublished until his death, for the result has been a one-sided and incomplete picture of the man, which it has taken much work like that of Legouis and Harper to correct; and it still needs some effort of the imagination to correct our impression of the older man, the author of *Ecclesiastical Sonnets* and what Byron called:

> A drowsy frowsy poem called *The Excursion*,
> Writ in a manner that is my aversion.

It is difficult to realise that there was in the younger Wordsworth a vein of Byron, at least of Shelley and Blake, a passionate lover, and an advocate, it may be, of free love. What makes him to many more interesting is that there was another strain in his strong northern nature which reacted against the revolutionary mood. If Wordsworth had told the whole story we might have understood the nature of that reaction, and see in it not only a gradual change in his political sentiments, a change which took place much more slowly than *The Prelude* suggests, but also a reaction of his somewhat Puritan temper from a Rousseauist, passionate mood into which he had been drawn for some time. Professor Legouis has, I think, wisely divined that the beautiful group of *Lucy* poems (whose heroine is, I fancy, an idealisation of his own sister Dorothy) express Wordsworth's sense of relief in escaping from a love of passion to a love of affection, affection for an English maiden:

> She dwelt among the untrodden ways
> Beside the springs of Dove,
> A Maid whom there were none to praise
> And very few to love:

A violet by a mossy stone
Half hidden from the eye!
Fair as a star, when only one
Is shining in the sky.

She lived unknown, and few could know
When Lucy ceased to be;
But she is in her grave, and, oh,
The difference to me!

. . . . . .

I travelled among unknown men
In lands beyond the sea;
Nor, England! did I know till then
What love I bore to thee.

'Tis past, that melancholy dream!
Nor will I quit thy shore
A second time; for still I seem
To love thee more and more.

Among thy mountains did I feel
The joy of my desire;
And she I cherished turned her wheel
Beside an English fire:

Thy mornings showed, thy nights concealed,
The bowers where Lucy played;
And thine too is the last green field
That Lucy's eyes surveyed.

That speaks the very soul of Wordsworth, and I have quoted it not only because of its relevance to the story of his earlier passion, but because it is the very quintessence, as we shall see, of Wordsworth's return to himself after the passions of the Revolution are over, his "illumination". France of the Revolution his mistress was; England and her morals, customs, prejudices became his wife.

But of this passionate episode in his life Wordsworth tells us nothing in *The Prelude*.[1] What is there chronicled at length is the process by which he came through the despondency which was for him, as for the Solitary, the consequence of the shattering of his high hopes for the emancipation of mankind. I need recall the stages in the briefest manner. It was not lightly that Wordsworth abandoned the "Good Cause", as Hazlitt called it. Like Milton, he was not to be at once dismayed by deeds of violence, whether the September Massacres or the murder of the King. Early in 1793, shortly after his return from France, he wrote a letter to Bishop Watson (but did not publish it) in defence of the Revolution. "At a moment big with the fate of the human race", he wrote, "I am sorry that you attach so much importance to the personal sufferings of the late royal

[1] But the experience is reflected in *Vaudracour and Julia*; and if the whole poem is not a success there are some lines in it enough to show that Wordsworth knew what it was to be in love as well as Burns or Byron or Shelley or any more vagrant lover:

> Earth breathed in one great presence of the spring;
> Life turned the meanest of her implements,
> Before his eyes, to price above all gold;
> The house she dwelt in was a sainted shrine;
> Her chamber-window did surpass in glory
> The portals of the dawn; all paradise
> Could, by the simple opening of a door,
> Let itself in upon him:—pathways, walks,
> Swarm'd with enchantment, till his spirit sank,
> Surcharg'd within him, overblest to move
> Beneath a sun that wakes a weary world
> To its dull round of ordinary cares:
> A man too happy for mortality.

The lines are not often included in anthologies of love-poetry. Yet I do not know in English poetry any better description of the flooding of love into a young and generous mind.

martyr, and that the present convulsions should not have prevented you from joining in the idle cry of modish lamentations that has resounded from the court to the cottage." One is reminded of Milton, busy while Charles was confronting his judges in composing his grim *Tenure of Kings and Magistrates*, and when the deed was done answering the royalist *Eikon Basilike* with the savage mockery of *Eikonoklastes*. But if Charles's death shocked the English people as profoundly as the death of Louis did a later age, Milton was the spokesman of the victorious party, and could say what he chose. Wordsworth had to be more cautious. The Government press was not at his disposal as it was at the older poet's, the literary champion of the regicides. But Wordsworth was no whit less intransigeant. When England went to war with France he prayed for the defeat of his countrymen.[1] Even through the reign of terror which

---

[1] At least he refused to join in prayer for them, and rejoiced in British defeats:

> I rejoiced,
> Yea, afterwards—truth most painful to record!—
> Exulted, in the triumph of my soul,
> When Englishmen by thousands were o'erthrown,
> Left without glory on the field or driven,
> Brave hearts! to shameful flight. It was a grief,—
> Grief call it not, 'twas anything but that,—
> A conflict of sensations without name,
> Of which *he* only, who may love the sight
> Of a village steeple, as I do, can judge,
> When, in the congregation bending all
> To their great Father, prayers were offered up,
> Or praises for our country's victories;
> And, mid the simple worshippers, perchance
> I only, like an uninvited guest
> Whom no one owned, sate silent, shall I add,
> Fed on the day of vengeance yet to come.

followed the attack by the Allies on France he held fast, and hailed the death of Robespierre[1] as a signal of returning sanity, a promise that the beneficent cause of emancipation, the realisation of the ideal of liberty, equality and fraternity, was to be renewed:

> In the people was my trust
> And in the virtues which mine eyes had seen.

It was when the French seemed to him to have belied the very *raison d'être* of the Revolution by the conquest of Switzerland that his sympathy with France died out, but not his democratic and republican principles. These endured for many years. As late as 1805 Sir George Beaumont warned Haydon that he must not be shocked

---

[1] How much the crimes of Robespierre and his gang haunted Wordsworth's imagination is told in an account of his dreams at this time. One or two of Wordsworth's dreams described in *The Prelude* are singularly vivid and might repay the study of the psychologist, e.g.:

> Sleep seized me, and I passed into a dream

in the earlier section, *Books*; and that during these terrible months:

> Most melancholy at that time, O Friend!
> Were my day-thoughts, my dreams were miserable;
> Through months, through years, long after the last beat
> Of those atrocities (I speak bare truth,
> As if to thee alone in private talk)
> I scarcely had one night of quiet sleep,
> Such ghastly visions had I of despair
> And tyranny, and implements of death,
> And long orations which in dreams I pleaded
> Before unjust Tribunals, with a voice
> Labouring, a brain confounded, and a sense
> Of treachery, and desertion in the place
> The holiest that I knew of, my own soul.

I have quoted here from the shorter, simpler version of 1805–6. We have supped so full of horrors since Wordsworth's time that our dreams have been less troubled by crueller deeds in Russia, Italy and Germany.

by Wordsworth's democratic views. What happened
was, that feeling made way for thought, for speculation:

> I had approached, like other youths, the shield
> Of human nature from the golden side,
> And would have fought even to the death to attest
> The quality of the metal which I saw.

Now he must make good intellectually what he had
accepted in an *élan* of the heart, caught up in the sweep
of a widespread wave of feeling. And so began that
painful process which some of us may have known,
if not in connection with political, at least with our
religious principles or prejudices, a process of subject-
ing everything to the scrutiny of a ruthless intellectual
analysis, a sensation as if one were tearing up feelings
and beliefs that have twined themselves about the very
fibres of the heart:

> So I fared
> Dragging all precepts, judgments, maxims, creeds,
> Like culprits to the bar; calling the mind,
> Suspiciously, to establish in plain day
> Her titles and her honours; now believing,
> Now disbelieving, endlessly perplexed
> With impulse, motive, right and wrong, the ground
> Of obligation, what the rule and whence
> The sanction; till, demanding formal *proof*
> And seeking it in everything, I lost
> All feeling of conviction, and, in fine,
> Sick, wearied out with contrarieties,
> Yielded up moral questions in despair.

It is through some such experience that Milton too
must have passed as it became clear that the victory of

the parliamentary party was not to mean the establishment of a free Church in a free State, as he drew away from his first Presbyterian allies, became the champion of regicide, at home and abroad, and began to subject to a fresh scrutiny the principles of government and the foundations of his religious beliefs in *The Tenure of Kings and Magistrates, Eikonoklastes, Defensio pro Populo Anglicano* (first and second), *A Way to Remove Hirelings out of the Church*, and finally the long hidden, late discovered *De Doctrinâ Christianâ*, in which Milton appears as so bold and individual a thinker, so remote from the orthodox Christianity of his day, Anglican, Presbyterian, Independent or Baptist. But Milton steered right on, however uncharted the seas, a Bolshevist in virtue alike of his intolerant temperament and his confident intellectualism. With Wordsworth it was otherwise. However far he had gone—and Wordsworth's battle, it must be remembered, was fought out privately, in his own soul or among his personal friends, Milton had taken the field, a David encountering that great Goliath, a Harapha, Salmasius, and carrying off the *spolia opima* before the admiring eyes of European scholarship—however far Wordsworth had gone and however obstinately he clung to his democratic tenets and sympathies, his was no Bolshevist temperament. He was no ruthless intellectual, following to its last consequence what the late Lord Salisbury called "the dead-reckoning of logic"; nor was his age such an intellectual era as the seventeenth century. The whole so-called Romantic Revival was a reaction against a too intellectual tradition. Even modern science was learning to trust more to observation and experiment than to the confident scholastic logic in which Milton still excelled. From the intellect Wordsworth turned to the senses and the imagination, from political speculation to the individual, to all the subtle but profound reactions of his emotional nature to its natural and human environment.

But Wordsworth's "conversion", as one may justly call it, had its deepest source in an individual, supernormal experience, his peculiarly profound sensuous and imaginative reaction to the natural scenery in which he had grown up by Esthwaite Lake and amid the hills of Cumberland and Westmorland. The little, somewhat tame lake of Esthwaite, perhaps as much as the more familiar Grasmere, has to some minds a measure of the fascination which clings to the Lake of Gennesaret, the Sea of Galilee. It has become an element in a spiritual and imaginative experience from which subsequent generations have drunk comfort if not healing.

For as Wordsworth came to himself, as under the influence of his wonderful sister Dorothy, and aided by the subtle (not to say at times sophistical) intellect of the great Coleridge, he began to see his way, "the master current" of his soul resumed its flow:

> And then he thinks he knows
> The hills where his life rose,
> And the sea where it goes.

For Wordsworth the source was the hills of his childhood, what he had there experienced, which now came back to his memory with a new significance. There is nothing, even in Wordsworth's poetry, nothing in any

poetry, quite like the descriptions, in the first books of
The Prelude, of the influence of natural scenery on the
senses of the boy and of the young man passing into
adolescence. In poignancy and fullness of feeling they
recall the few personal passages in *Paradise Lost*. But
the feeling which they express is a very different one and
demands a more careful analysis. It is more in the nature
of the prophetic, intuitive feeling of which I have spoken,
for in that feeling Wordsworth found, after his period of
"Sturm und Drang", a message for himself and the world.

Mr Garrod has contended, and not unjustly, that it
was an effect purely of the senses; and that is true up to
a certain point. Let me take what seems to me the
purest expression of this intense consciousness of the
beauty and the life of nature, the purest in the sense that
there is no intellectual reaction, no endeavour under the
influence of the feeling to interpret, to give it a prophetic significance such as I shall illustrate later:

> The sands of Westmoreland, the creeks and bays
> Of Cumbria's rocky limits, they can tell
> How, when the Sea threw off his evening shade,
> And to the shepherd's hut on distant hills
> Sent welcome notice of the rising moon,
> How I have stood, to fancies such as these
> A stranger, linking with the spectacle
> No conscious memory of a kindred sight,
> And bringing with me no peculiar sense
> Of quietness or peace; yet have I stood,
> Even while mine eye hath moved o'er many a league
> Of shining water, gathering as it seemed
> Through every hair-breadth in that field of light
> New pleasure like a bee among the flowers.

Or again it is not every boy who, returning from a day of gaiety in the country, has felt as Wordsworth feels in this passage:

> But, ere night-fall,
> When in our pinnace we returned at leisure
> Over the shadowy lake, and to the beach
> Of some small island steered our course with one,
> The Minstrel of the Troop, and left him there,
> And rowed off gently, while he blew his flute
> Alone upon the rock—oh, then the calm
> And dead still water lay upon my mind
> Even with a weight of pleasure, and the sky,
> Never before so beautiful, sank down
> Into my heart, and held me like a dream.

The skating scene is of the same quality, massive but vague, at once sensuous and visionary:

> So through the darkness and the cold we flew,
> And not a voice was idle; with the din
> Smitten, the precipices rang aloud;
> The leafless trees and every icy crag
> Tinkled like iron; while far distant hills
> Into the tumult sent an alien sound
> Of melancholy not unnoticed, while the stars
> Eastward were sparkling clear, and in the west
> The orange sky of evening died away.
> .   .   .   .   .   And oftentimes,
> When we had given our bodies to the wind,
> And all the shadowy banks on either side
> Came sweeping through the darkness, spinning still
> The rapid line of motion, then at once
> Have I, reclining back upon my heels,
> Stopped short; yet still the solitary cliffs
> Wheeled by me—even as if the earth had rolled
> With visible motion her diurnal round!

> Behind me did they stretch in solemn train,
> Feebler and feebler, and I stood and watched
> Till all was tranquil as a dreamless sleep.

Wordsworth's experience is primarily a sensuous one. So far I think Mr Garrod is right. But note its peculiar sensuous quality. It is not sights and sounds as such, still less warmth and odour and all the other varieties (as they are) of the sense of touch. Wordsworth is not a sensuous poet as that term is applicable to such lines as these from Keats:

> I cannot see what flowers are at my feet,
>   Nor what soft incense hangs upon the boughs,
> But, in embalmed darkness, guess each sweet
>   Wherewith the seasonable month endows
> The grass, the thicket, and the fruit-tree wild;
>   White hawthorn and the pastoral eglantine,
> Fast fading violets cover'd up in leaves;
>   And mid-May's eldest child,
> The coming musk-rose, full of dewy wine,
>   The murmurous haunt of flies on Summer eves—

or other passages that I might cite from Milton, Shakespeare, Shelley, Tennyson, as well as Keats. Even the austere Milton has passages of more properly sensuous writing. Wordsworth himself describes the peculiar nature of his consciousness when he says, a few lines before my first extract:

>   Even then
> I held unconscious intercourse with beauty
> Old as creation, drinking in a pure
> Organic pleasure from the silver wreaths
> Of curling mist, or from the level plain
> Of waters coloured by impending clouds.

"Organic pleasure", that is the right word. The foundation of Wordsworth's peculiar sense of nature was his own organic sense of well-being, combined with an imagination which transferred this sense of life and well-being to the objects of inanimate nature. He saw and felt the beauty of the scenery amid which he lived, as others of his companions doubtless did; but to his deep sensibility, his strong and healthy sense of life, this beauty became more than sensuous beauty. It became as it were the outward manifestation, the expressive countenance of a life as full, as intense, as joyous as his own, but greater, sublimer. And accordingly, in other of these descriptions, the pleasure is not so purely sensuous and imaginative; it unites itself with other feelings, other aspects of the life of the soul, moral, e.g. as when he tells us of his experience in robbing a friend's traps set for birds:

> Sometimes it befel
> In these night wanderings, that a strong desire
> O'erpowered my better reason, and the bird
> Which was the captive of another's toil
> Became my prey; and when the deed was done
> I heard among the solitary hills
> Low breathings coming after me, and sounds
> Of undistinguishable motions, steps
> Almost as silent as the turf they trod.

Or when he stole the boat:

> One summer evening, etc.[1]

And the moral deepens into the religious in that intense

---

[1] *The Prelude*, Book 1. Notice the sequence. He had stolen, for the time, the boat:

> It was an act of stealth
> And troubled pleasure, etc.

moment when, returning from a night of frivolity and dancing, he saw the sun rise:

> Magnificent
> The morning rose, in memorable pomp,

and it is surely his conscience that makes the sudden appearance of the huge peak so awe-inspiring:

> I struck and struck again,
> And growing still in stature, the grim shape
> Towered up between me and the stars, and still,
> For so it seemed, with purpose of its own
> And measured motion like a living thing,
> Strode after me. With trembling oars I turned,
> And through the silent water stole my way
> Back to the covert of the willow tree;
> There in her mooring-place I left my bark, etc.

Wordsworth's reaction in each of these instances is a weaker form of Macbeth's to the consciousness that he has done the murder:

> "Methought I heard a voice cry 'Sleep no more!
> Macbeth does murder sleep', ꞌtc."

> "Still it cried 'Sleep no more!' to all the house:
> 'Glamis hath murdered sleep, and therefore Cawdor
> Shall sleep no more, Macbeth shall sleep no more.' "

So at least I have read Wordsworth's lines. Mr Aldous Huxley has another reading of the incident. He does not connect the apparition of the peak and its influence on Wordsworth with the theft of the boat. For him it is an instance of Nature's refusal to "partake of our moods". "She turns round on the human spectator and gives him something utterly unlike his gift to her, reveals herself as a being marvellously and beautifully, or else more often terrifyingly, alien from man. In one of the finest passages of *The Prelude* Wordsworth has recorded this most disquieting experience", and he quotes the passage at length. One hesitates to differ from so fine a poet and critic as Mr Huxley, yet I confess that to me the incident appears to describe an experience in which Nature *does* reflect our moods, the spot upon the brain shows itself without, Nature takes on herself the guardianship of the moral law; the "craggy steep" becomes to Wordsworth a paler reflection of what Mount Sinai had been to the Israelites: "And it came to pass on the third day, when it was morning, that there were thunders and lightnings, and a thick cloud upon the mount, and the voice of a trumpet exceeding loud; and all the people that was in the camp trembled." But to a modern writer the word "moral" is a red rag.

Glorious as e'er I had beheld—in front
The sea lay laughing at a distance; near,
The solid mountains shone, bright as the clouds,
Grain-tinctured, drenched in empyrean light;
And in the meadows and the lower grounds
Was all the sweetness of a common dawn—
Dews, vapours, and the melody of birds,
And labourers going forth to till the fields.
Ah! need I say, dear Friend! that to the brim
My heart was full; I made no vows, but vows
Were then made for me; bond unknown to me
Was given, that I should be, else sinning greatly,
A dedicated Spirit. On I walked
In thankful blessedness, which yet survives.

These were the experiences on the memory of which Wordsworth, discarding Godwin and political or moral theorising, turned back to recover the sense of joy and well-being which he had lost. It was his own deep sense of well-being, of joy, which he had communicated to the world that seemed to him to be renewing its youth in the revolution in France when he felt it a joy to be alive and to be young very heaven. That joy had failed him, and he had lost his way in the perplexities of analysis and speculation till:

Sick, wearied out with contrarieties,

he

Yielded up moral questions in despair.

But fundamentally Wordsworth was, as he admits, "a happy man", and his temperament asserting itself carried him back to these early experiences so full of deep joy, and not only that, for they seemed to him now to contain an answer to his perplexities. It was joy that

he had sought, that all of us are always seeking, in however diverse ways, led by whatever Will o' the Wisps it
may be. Wordsworth and his generation had followed
one of these, a glittering spirit which called itself
"Liberty, Equality, and Fraternity", and it had led to
the Reign of Terror and Napoleon Bonaparte, and for
Wordsworth to the dusty purlieus of Godwin's *Political
Justice*; and now in a different manner he realised that
happiness was to be sought:

> Not in Utopia—subterranean fields—
> Or some secreted island Heaven knows where,
> But in the very world, which is the world
> Of all of us—the place where in the end
> We find our happiness or not at all.

Wordsworth, in the years from about 1797 to about
1803, was like one who has been converted, or who has
recovered his faith, and the poems he wrote are read
with most understanding and enjoyment if one reads
them as the outpourings of such a convert, a convales-
cent, the joy of a recovered faith in God which for
Wordsworth is in Nature:

> I heard a thousand blended notes,
> While in a grove I sate reclined,
> In that sweet mood when pleasant thoughts
> Bring sad thoughts to the mind.

And again:

> It is the first mild day of March:
> Each minute sweeter than before,
> The red-breast sings from the tall larch
> That stands beside our door.

12*

There is a blessing in the air,
Which seems a sense of joy to yield
To the bare trees, and mountains bare,
And grass in the green field.

And

The sun, above the mountain's head,
A freshening lustre mellow
Through all the long green fields has spread,
His first sweet evening yellow.

Books! 'tis a dull and endless strife;
Come, hear the woodland linnet,
How sweet his music! on my life,
There's more of wisdom in it.

One impulse from a vernal wood
May teach you more of man,
Of moral evil and of good,
Than all the sages can.

And

My eyes are dim with childish tears,
My heart is idly stirred,
For the same sound is in my ears
Which in those days I heard.

The blackbird amid leafy trees,
The lark above the hill,
Let loose their carols when they please,
Are quiet when they will.

With Nature never do they wage
A foolish strife; they see
A happy youth, and their old age
Is beautiful and free.

That is to me the essential Wordsworth, a poet of
joy, of recovered joy, of joy drawn from the purest of
sources. But one must read them as poetry, not as

philosophical dogmas, as if Wordsworth maintained seriously that an impulse from a vernal wood made unnecessary any study of Aristotle's *Ethics* or Butler's *Sermons* or the Bible or any other source from which one may choose to draw practical directions for the moral life. Wordsworth's hyperboles are of the same kind as Steele's about the lady he loved, that to love her is a liberal education; but they are more than that, they are, at what level of approximation I will not attempt to determine, of the same kind as the Hebrew prophets' exultant declarations that God is a God of Justice and Mercy to whom the passing of one's children through the fire is an abomination, whose demand is that "judgement shall roll down as waters, and righteousness as a mighty stream". They are intuitions, born of feeling, thought, and experience, and from them the reason, working more abstractly, may draw erroneous as well as just inferences as to special circumstances. But of that later when I come to consider the link Wordsworth finds between Nature and Man.

For Wordsworth was, of course, not content to be thought, or to be, a poet of Nature only, singing the sensuous and emotional joy of a life lived in natural surroundings, like Cowper in *The Task*:

God made the country, and Man made the town.

Wordsworth desired to be a philosophical poet, whose ultimate theme was not Nature but the heart of Man. And so in *The Prelude* we are told at considerable length how Man gradually took his place in the natural scenery which the poet loved so passionately, and in the

famous lines written above Tintern Abbey we are assured that:

> I have learned
> To look on Nature, not as in the hour
> Of thoughtless youth; but hearing oftentimes
> The still, sad music of humanity,
> Nor harsh, nor grating, though of ample power
> To chasten and subdue.

It was Man rather than individual men, a sublime feature
of the hills and valleys amid which he loved and worked:

> A rambling schoolboy thus
> I felt his presence in his own domain
> As of a lord and master, or a power
> Or genius, under Nature, under God,
> Presiding; and severest solitude
> Had more commanding looks when he was there.

Men made the same sort of appeal to him as Nature did,
an appeal more to the imagination than the heart,
though in his way he loved them. His disposition was
the opposite of Swift's, who loved individuals but hated
the race. What appealed to Wordsworth in the men and
women and children whom he had known in these
earliest years, as he turned back to them in memory
from the dry husks of Godwinian analysis, was just
those things which are least intellectual, most akin to
great natural forces, their primitive unreasoned instincts
as love of property, or love of country, the elemental
strength of a mother's love as in *The Affliction of Margaret*, of a father's in *Michael*, or the affection that
unites two brothers in *The Brothers* — these things,
and also the elemental simplicity of their lives, the
regular succession of tasks in the shepherd's life, as

regular as the succession of day and night, Winter and Summer, and as unquestioning. It was this in the life of Nature and the life and feelings of the peasantry which filled him with a renewed and deepened sense of joy, this regular, inevitable, unquestioning fulfilment of an allotted function. The stars in their unchanging courses, the patient hills that stand up uncomplaining alike to sun and storm, the days and seasons in their recurrence, the birds and flowers and clouds—these it seems to Wordsworth neither question nor rebel nor grow weary, and thereby it seemed to the poet's interpreting, personifying imagination, their life is not only beautiful, but filled with a profound sense of joy, a joy which men might share if they too could discover the law of *their* being, and fulfil it unmurmuringly. Impulse and law, these are the foci of life. Life is fullest and most joyous when a powerful impulse flows strongly and unchecked in the course prescribed for it by the law of an organic creature's being. That is true of spiritual as of physical life, and what Wordsworth's poetry would have us learn, is to learn from Nature, from simpler beings than our own, this secret of the joy he finds in Nature:

> Through primrose tufts, in that green bower,
> The periwinkle trailed its wreaths;
> And 'tis my faith that every flower
> Enjoys the air it breathes.

> The birds around me hopped and played,
> Their thoughts I cannot measure:—
> But the least motion which they made,
> It seemed a thrill of pleasure.

So might man live if he would trust what are the

native instincts of *his* heart—faith and reverence and love:

> Ye motions of delight that haunt the sides
> Of the green hills; ye breezes and soft airs
> Whose subtle intercourse with breathing flowers
> Feelingly watched might teach man's haughty race
> How without injury to take, to give
> Without offence.

> By love subsists
> All lasting grandeur, by pervading love:
> That gone we are as dust.

And this is the link which connects Wordsworth's poems expressive of his own feelings for Nature, the visionary ecstasies of his youth described in the early books of *The Prelude*, the recovered joy of the *Lyrical Ballads*, with those poems the subject of which is incidents in the life of men. I need not retrace the steps by which, as recorded in the autobiographical poem, he made his way from his love of Nature to his love of man. These are perhaps to some extent reconstructed *a posteriori*. The important thing is the relation in which they finally stood to one another. How far and in what way is Wordsworth a poet not of nature but of humanity? What was the answer he found to the problems raised by the Revolution, the subsequent disappointment, and the study of Godwin?

Wordsworth's intense individual reaction to the influence of the scenery in which he grew up had its origin, I have said following Mr Garrod, in an exceptionally acute sensibility, organic rather than of the individual senses, reacting on his imagination. But another idiosyncracy of the poet throughout his life, one

which outlived his intenser reactions to natural scenery,
was the strength of his affections. Of an early school
companion he writes:

> My morning walks
> Were early;—oft, before the hours of school ·
> I travell'd round our little lake, five miles
> Of pleasant wandering.   Happy time! more dear
> For this, that one was by my side, a Friend,
> *Then passionately loved.*

This proneness to passionate attachments, affections,
persisted throughout his life—for his brother, his sister,
his daughter to whose marriage he could not bring himself to consent without acute suffering. The death of
each of his children left a scar. It is in connection with
this side of his nature that one realises how much has
been lost by the absence of a history of his love for
Annette. Whatever one may think of Mr Read's attempt
to explain the whole of Wordsworth's life from the
effects of this experience about which we know nothing,
it is impossible to deny that wanting it the story told
in *The Prelude* is incomplete, for the main theme of
Wordsworth's poems of incidents in human life is love,
the workings of love, its power to inflict the deepest
wounds and to heal the most irreparable. His optimism,
of which so much is said, seems at times like the
optimism of King Lear:

> Thence may I select
> Sorrow, that is not sorrow, but delight,
> And miserable love, that is not pain
> To hear of, for the glory that redounds
> Therefrom to human kind, and what we are.

There is a comfort in the strength of love;
'Twill make a thing endurable which else
Would overset the brain, or break the heart.

It makes death welcome to Lear, and the fate of Cordelia
and Lear endurable to us, "delight to hear of". In Professor Lane Cooper's *Concordance to the Poems of William
Wordsworth* (London, 1911) the word "Nature" (and
to avoid complications I will include varieties as "native", "naturally", etc.) occupies some eight columns.
The word "Love" (including likewise parts of the verb,
compounds, and derivatives as "lovely", etc.) occupies
no fewer than thirteen. And leaving aside for a moment
the question of treatment, diction, etc., what is the
theme of poems such as *Goody Blake and Harry Gill,
Simon Lee, The Thorn, The Last of the Flock, The Mad
Mother, The Idiot Boy, The Complaint of a Forsaken Indian
Woman*, all in *Lyrical Ballads*, but love, its intensity in
a mother, its reactions when slighted or wronged? His
declared purpose was to "make these incidents and
situations interesting by tracing in them, truly though
not ostentatiously, the primary laws of our nature chiefly
as far as regards the manner in which we associate ideas
in a state of excitement". So pedantically can he talk
when following Coleridge and Hartley he tries to explain what is moving him. In these poems too he was led
astray by other theories, *e.g.* of poetic diction, and, worse
than the theories, by the choice of a wrong model for
simplicity, the ballad, not the older traditional genuine
ballad, but the banal broadside ballads, "dull, long-
drawn out, and didactic".

But the same theme, love not as passion in the

narrower sense of the word but passionate affection, its "wily subtleties and refluxes", this is what Wordsworth is in quest of in later and finer poems: *Michael*, *The Brothers*, *Margaret*, *The Affliction of Margaret*, *Ruth*, *The Happy Warrior*, *The White Doe of Rylstone*; and to these should be added the tales told by the Parson in *The Excursion*, and yet more the patriotic sonnets, for Wordsworth's poems are not patriotic in the same sense as Scott's or Campbell's. Their theme is not the glories of war, but the heart of man, its ardours and endurances. And this poetry of the heart of Man is in fact closely bound up with the poetry of Nature, for his treatment of Nature had never been merely descriptive and inanimate. It had always been essentially human.[1] He lent his own sense of life to things or, to put it otherwise, in a prophetic intuition he apprehended the law of nature as ultimately the law of love. For what

---

[1] No incident that met his eyes in London touched him more deeply than the father with the sickly child:

> 'Twas a Man
> Whom I saw sitting in an open Square
> Close to an iron paling that fenced in
> The spacious grass-plot; on the corner stone
> Of the low wall in which the pales were fix'd
> Sate this one man, and with a sickly babe
> Upon his knee, whom he had thither brought
> For sunshine, and to breathe the fresher air.
> Of those who pass'd, and me who look'd at him,
> He took no note; but in his brawny arms
> (The artificer was to the elbow bare
> And from his work this moment had been stolen)
> He held the child, and, bending over it,
> As if he were afraid both of the sun
> And of the air which he had come to seek,
> *He eyed it with unutterable love.*
>   *The Prelude*, VIII. 843–58 (1805).

is law in the inorganic, and a great part of the organic, world is in the free nature of man Duty, and Duty is ultimately the law of Love:

> Flowers laugh before thee in their beds,
> And fragrance in thy footing treads;
> Thou dost preserve the stars from wrong;
And the most ancient heavens through thee are fresh and strong.

But:
> Serene will be our days and bright,
> And happy will our natures be,
> When love is an unerring light,
> And joy its own security.

That is Wordsworth's poetic or prophetic intuition corresponding, in what degree each reader will decide for himself, to the Hebrew prophets' intuition that the only true God is a God of righteousness and mercy to whom the passing of one's children through the fire is an abomination and whose desire is that "Judgement roll down as waters, and righteousness in a mighty stream". Neither can be deduced by human ratiocination from the face of things as they are or as science reveals them. It may be, as Mr Aldous Huxley contends, that a visit to a tropic forest would have disturbed Wordsworth's faith in Nature. Fear precludes all other emotions for the time being: but fear is no more than joy, if as much, the final measure of truth. Nor have more dangerous aspects of Nature than the Lake District deprived of their love of Nature such men as Hudson or Schweitzer. In any case Mr Huxley himself, a man apparently as sensitive as Swift to the bad smells, physical and moral, that haunt human life and to which most of us grow perhaps too much inured, has, it would seem, come to a conclusion about life and how it may be made better that does not differ essentially from that of Milton and Wordsworth. For Milton too love is the fulfilling of the law:

> The Law of God exact he shall fulfill
> Both by obedience and by love, *though love*
> *Alone fulfill the Law.*   P.L. XII, 402–5.

But his temperament and experience had laid the stress on will, the need of strength of will. And Mr Huxley in passing from his revolting picture of mankind conditioned by science and in the interest of industry to a dream of men freely conditioning themselves[1] finds that love is the end, but that love to become perfect must undergo the strenuous and sustained training of the will, the Will to Love. "Wherefore the law (i.e. the will) was our schoolmaster to bring us unto Christ, that we might be justified by faith (love). But after that faith (love) is come, we are no longer under a schoolmaster."

Milton as an artist is altogether a larger and more splendid luminary in the poetic heaven than Wordsworth. He is the supreme master of poetic evolution and poetic diction—a style sensuous, impassioned, elaborate, musical, a very cloth of gold. From the *Nativity* and *At a Solemn Music* to *Paradise Regained* and *Samson Agonistes* everything that Milton wrote is such that no word could well be altered without marring the consciously yet exquisitely artistic structure of the whole, without producing a discord in the organ-like harmonies in which each word is a pealing note. But though form

[1] Compare *Brave New World* (1932) with its sequel, *Eyeless in Gaza* (1936).

is the *sine qua non* of poetry it is not the whole. The
beautiful form must reflect a beautiful soul. Is it not
with poems as with people? Many an almost plain face
through which shine "love, sweetness, goodness" wins
us more in the long run than features of more perfect
contour, greater but colder dignity of outline. Now no
one will deny to Milton's poetry grandeur of soul as
well as perfection of art, but is not the soul a little
narrow and self-centred in its grandeur and intensity?
Sublime Milton's poetry is, in spirit and form. All
things go hand in hand to evoke admiration and awe—
great scenes, great persons, great issues, great passions,
and a great style, "the grand style". Nor are there
wanting solemn touches of noble pathos, as when in
language of unsurpassed beauty and pathos and dignity
he speaks of his blindness:

> Thus with the year
> Seasons return; but not to me returns
> Day, or the sweet approach of even or morn,
> Or sight of vernal bloom, or Summer's rose,
> Or flocks, or herds, or human face divine.

Or in that sonnet—which Dr Johnson thought poor—
where he bewails the death of his second wife:

> Methought I saw my late espoused saint,
>
> . . . .
>
> But oh! as to embrace me she inclined,
> I waked, she fled, and day brought back my night.

But these are personal touches, and the last stands
alone. What we miss in Milton with all his greatness is
sympathy with poor human nature—its blended greatness and weakness. His attitude to us is harsh and

dictatorial; and it is here that Wordsworth supplies what we seek in vain in Milton. Wordsworth's sympathy with human nature was intense if somewhat narrow in range. It may be true that "large tracts of human feeling and experience were unvisited by him and lay beyond his horizon". But his narrowness is not that of arrogance or conscious superiority. He loves his fellowmen with such intensity—is so full of his message of joy and peace—that he is indifferent to aspects of their life irrelevant to his great purpose. He has not Shakespeare's or Burns's interest in the manners of men, he is so deeply interested in their souls; and like Milton he lacks humour. But his heart goes out to humanity like that of the great prophets. If he loves Nature it is as an inspirer of life and joy; his Nature is in profoundest sympathy with the nature of the human spirit. She is a great personality, a "Commissary of God", in whose life he finds the joy he would wake in man. "The Flowers", the "Sylvan Wye", "Poor Susan", Matthew in all his changing moods, "Michael" and "Margaret", the peasants of the Tyrol—are all moved by one spirit—Love:

That moves the Sun in Heaven and all the Stars.

Of love in a great but restricted sense of the word Wordsworth had, as we have seen, comparatively little to say—romantic love—

Love unconquerable, who makest havoc of men's wealth, who keepest thy vigil in the soft cheeks of a maiden—(Sophocles)—

the love of the songs of Donne and Burns and Sappho and Catullus. That element Wordsworth seems to have cut out of his life early. But love in St Paul's sense of "caritas" that "beareth all things, believeth all things, hopeth all things, endureth all things"—sympathy with his fellow-men and desire for their welfare—that is the key-note of all his poetry, the source and inspiration of the joy of which he sings:

> Love now a universal birth
> From heart to heart is stealing.

> And you must love him ere to you
> He will seem worthy of your love,

and of the pathos of *The Ruined Cottage*, of *Michael*, of *The Brothers*, of *The Affliction of Margaret*. Wordsworth we think of principally as a poet of Nature, but that is an incomplete view. He is, at the centre, one of the great poets of love. With Shelley he finds in love the ultimate solution of the problem of life; but he has not Shelley's impatience, nor Milton's intellectuality. The value of his poetry is not in deductions that may be made from his central intuitions of the life of Nature and the Heart of Man, but in the intuitions themselves.

REFERENCES TO QUOTATIONS

Unless otherwise stated, all references in this list to Milton's works are to volumes of the Columbia University edition

Pp. 1–2. Goldsmith. *The Citizen of the World*, Letter xcvi.

Pp. 3–4. Horace, *Carmina*, ii. 18, and Shakespeare, *Macbeth*, v. 5. 19 ff.

P. 5. Dryden, *Religio Laici*, 453–4.

Pp. 5–6. Grierson, *Metaphysical Poetry*, p. xxviii.

P. 7. Jeremiah xx. 7, 9 (R.V.).

P. 8. Eckerman, *Conversations of Goethe*, trans. John Oxenford. Bell and Sons, 1874, pp. 234–5, and Amos v. 21–4.

P. 9. *Intimations of Immortality*, and Micah vi. 6–8.

P. 10. *Some Passages in the Life and Death of John Earl of Rochester, etc.* London, M.DCC.LXXXVII, pp. 56–7.

Pp. 14–15. Jeremiah xliv. 15–18.

P. 16. Isaiah x. 5–6.

P. 17. Hosea xiv. 1–9, and Shelley, *Julian and Maddalo*, ll. 172–6.

P. 18. Isaiah xi. 1–9 and lxi. 1–2.

Pp. 19–20. Jeremiah xxxi. 1–9, and Shelley, *Prometheus Unbound*, ll. 400–11.

Pp. 20–1. Robertson Smith, *The Prophets of Israel*, 1882, p. 219.

P. 21. Isaiah v. 1–7.

Pp. 23–4. Crabbe, *The World of Dreams*.

Pp. 26–7. Milton, *The Reason of Church Government*, vol. iii, pp. 238–9.

P. 27. *Apology for Smectymnuus*, vol. iii, pp. 287 and 303–4.

P. 28. *Of Education*, vol. iv, p. 286.

Pp. 28–9. *Paradise Lost*, book vii, ll. 1–12 and 30–9.

P. 30–1. *The Reason of Church Government*, vol. iv, pp. 230–1.

P. 33. *Areopagitica*, vol. iv, p. 340, and *Of Reformation*, vol. iii, pp. 78–9.

Pp. 34–5. *Animadversions upon the Remonstrants Defence, etc.*, vol. iii, pp. 145–8.

Pp. 35–6. Isaiah lxiii–lxiv end.

Pp. 38–9. *Animadversions upon the Remonstrants Defence, etc.*, vol. iii, p. 107, and *The Reason of Church Government*, vol. iii, p. 231, and *Of Reformation*, vol. iii, p. 79.

Pp. 41–2. *The Reason of Church Government, The Second Book*, vol. iii, p. 246, and *Of Reformation, The First Book*, vol. iii, p. 35.

Pp. 43–4. *Of Reformation*, vol. iii, pp. 1–4.

P. 45. *The Reason of Church Government, The Second Book*, chap. III, vol. III, pp. 259–61. Compare with this, especially the sentence beginning "And although I have given it the name of a liquid," Marvell's poem *On a Drop of Dew*.

P. 46. *Ibid*. pp. 261–2.

P. 50. "It is better to marry, etc." The Roman Catholic doctrine of marriage starts from this seventh chapter of the Epistle to the Corinthians. "As pastors should propose to themselves the happy and perfect lives of the Christian people, their most earnest wish must be that of the Apostle, when writing to the Corinthians in these words: I would that you were all even as myself...that is that all would observe the virtue of continence; for the faithful can find no greater happiness in this life than that the soul, distracted by no worldly care, and every unruly desire of the flesh being tranquillized and extinguished, repose in the sole study of piety, and the contemplation of heavenly things. But since, as the same Apostle testifies, every one hath his proper gift from God, one after this manner, and another after that...and marriage is adorned with great and divine blessings so as truly and properly to be numbered among the sacraments of the Catholic Church, etc." Dr Donovan, *Catechism of the Council of Trent* (1914), p. 291. To an outsider this, perhaps wrongly, seems to imply that, though a sacrament, marriage is a concession to human weakness. One had thought that St Paul spoke as a missionary expecting the early Coming of Christ.

P. 52. *The Doctrine and Discipline of Divorce, etc., The First Book*, chap. V, part II, vol. III, pp. 399–400; and *ibid., The Second Book*, chap. XVII, p. 485, and *The First Book*, chap. III, p. 397.

P. 53. *Ibid., The Second Book*, chap. XX, p. 496.

P. 54. *Of Education*, vol. IV, p. 277.

P. 56. David Masson: *Life of John Milton, etc.* (1873), vol. III, pp. 186–7.

P. 57. *Colasterion*, vol. IV, p. 273.

Pp. 67–8. *A Letter to a Friend, Concerning the Ruptures of the Commonwealth*, vol. VI, pp. 101–2.

P. 68. The quotations on this and other pages from the *Defensio Secunda* are taken from the translation by Robert Fellowes, A.M. (Oxon) (1771–1847), printed in J. A. St John's *The Prose Works of Milton* (1848), vol. I, and at the end of the prose part of *The Complete Works Prose and Poetical of John Milton*, with an introduction by Robert Fletcher (London, 1875). The prose works of Milton appealed strongly to the ardent Liberals of the nineteenth century, especially among the dissenters. For the Latin text with a new translation, more accurate perhaps but less idiomatic and vigorous, see the Columbia University edition, vol. VIII.

Pp. 69–70 note. See Columbia University edition, vol. x, pp. 318–25.

P. 81. *Paradise Lost*, book xii, ll. 537–51.

P. 82. *Ibid.*, book viii, ll. 533–4.

P. 83. *Donne's Poetical Works*, ed. Grierson (1912), vol. i, p. 200.

P. 84. Spenser: *Colin Clouts come home again*.

P. 88. *Donne's Poetical Works*, vol. i, pp. 336–7.

P. 96. My citations of the *De Doctrina* here and on the following pages are taken from the translation by Charles R. Sumner, as given with the Latin text on the opposite pages, in the Columbia University edition, vols. xv, xvi and xvii.

P. 99 note. *Paradise Lost*, ed. Thomas Newton, D.D. (1749), vol. i, pp. 358–9.

P. 100. William Cowper, Olney Hymns xv, *Praise for the Fountain Opened*. Zechariah xiii. 1, and Crawshaw, *Upon the Bleeding Crucifix, A Song*.

P. 102. *De Doctrina*, chap. xxv, vol. xvi, pp. 75–6.

P. 104. *Paradise Lost*, book xii, ll. 469–78.

P. 106. For Milton's full doctrine of God see *De Doctrina*, chap. ii, pp. 25–61. God is incomprehensible, but the statements about Him in the Scriptures are to be taken quite literally. "Our safest way is to form in our minds such a conception of God as shall correspond with His own delineation and representation of Himself in the sacred writings....If it repented Jehovah that He had made man. Gen. vi. 6...let us believe that it did repent Him, only taking care to remember that...repentance when applied to God does not arise from inadvertency as in men; for so He himself has cautioned us, Num. xxiii. 19. God is not a man that He should repent etc." It seems to me an attempt to combine the theological transcendence with the literal acceptance of the Scriptures, and in Milton's poem the effect is to lose the sublime transcendence, remoteness, of Dante's vision and the sublime passionate humanity, angry and loving, of the God of the Hebrew poets.

P. 130. Gray to West, April [1742]. It is noteworthy that none of Dryden's "poetic diction" here cited comes from Milton, unless it be "smouldering" and "beldam", and both these are from early poems, *Vacation Exercise* and the *Hymn*. Dryden has sought his effects rather by archaising, like Spenser, than by Latinisms. Milton uses "loose array" of an army, Dryden, *Flower and the Leaf*, l. 35, of dress. Milton uses the adjective "boon", not the noun meaning "prayer". Pope borrows from Dryden, Gray says. The *O.E.D.* generally cited the Pope, ignoring the Dryden.

P. 140. *Samson Agonistes*, ll. 293–314, 322.

PRINTED IN GREAT BRITAIN BY
LOWE & BRYDONE PRINTERS LTD., LONDON, N.W.10